JOHN F.
KENNEDY

PRESIDENTS
and their
DECISIONS

JOHN F. KENNEDY

Book Editors:

TOM LANSFORD, PH.D.
UNIVERSITY OF SOUTHERN MISSISSIPPI

ROBERT P. WATSON, PH.D.
FLORIDA ATLANTIC UNIVERSITY

BONNIE SZUMSKI, *Publisher*
SCOTT BARBOUR, *Managing Editor*

GREENHAVEN
PRESS®

THOMSON
GALE

San Diego • Detroit • New York • San Francisco • Cleveland
New Haven, Conn. • Waterville, Maine • London • Munich

THOMSON
★
GALE

LIBRARY OF CONGRESS CATALOGING-IN-PUBLICATION DATA

John F. Kennedy / Tom Lansford and Robert P. Watson, book editors.
p. cm. — (Presidents and their decisions)
Includes bibliographical references and index.
ISBN 0-7377-1112-4 (lib. : alk. paper) — ISBN 0-7377-1111-6 (pbk. : alk. paper)
1. Kennedy, John F. (John Fitzgerald), 1917–1963. United States—Politics and government—1961–1963—Decision making. 3. United States—Foreign relations—1961–1963—Decision making. 4. Presidents—United States—Biography. I. Lansford, Tom. III. Series. II. Watson, Robert P., 1962– .
E841.J57 2004
973.922'092—dc22   2003061670

CONTENTS

Chapter 2: Human Rights and Peace

Chapter 3: Civil Rights

Chapter 5: Managing the Press

FOREWORD

"THE PRESIDENCY OF THE UNITED STATES IS OFTEN DE-scribed as the most powerful office in the world," writes Forrest McDonald in *The American Presidency: An Intellectual History.* "In one sense this description is accurate," he says, "for even casual decisions made in the White House can affect the lives of millions of people." But McDonald also notes that presidential power "is restrained by the countervailing power of Congress, the courts, the bureaucracy, popular opinion, the news media, and state and local governments. What presidents do have is awesome responsibilities combined with unique opportunities to persuade others to do their bidding—opportunities enhanced by the possibility of dispensing favors, by the mystique of presidential power, and by the aura of monarchy that surrounds the president."

The way various presidents have used the complex power of their office is the subject of Greenhaven Press's Presidents and Their Decisions series. Each volume in the series examines one particular president and the key decisions he made while in office.

Some presidential decisions have been made in a relatively brief period of time, as with Abraham Lincoln's suspension of the writ of habeus corpus at the start of the Civil War. Others were refined as they were implemented over a period of years, as was the case with Franklin Delano Roosevelt's struggle to lead the country out of the Great Depression. Some presidential actions are generally lauded by historians—for example, Lyndon Johnson's support of the civil rights movement in the 1960s—while others have been condemned—such as Richard Nixon's efforts, from 1972 to 1974, to cover up the involvement of his aides in the Watergate scandal.

Most of the truly history-making presidential decisions, though, remain the subject of intense scrutiny and historical debate. Many of these were made during a time of war or other crisis, in which a president was forced to risk either spectacular success or devastating failure. Examples include Lincoln's much-scrutinized handling of the crisis at Fort Sumter, the first conflict of the Civil War; FDR's efforts to aid the European Allies at the beginning of World War II; Harry Truman's controversial decision to use the atomic bomb in order to end that conflict; and Lyndon Johnson's fateful decision to escalate the war in Vietnam.

Each volume in the Presidents and Their Decisions series devotes a full chapter to each of the president's key decisions. The essays in each chapter, most written by presidential historians and biographers, offer a range of perspectives on the president and his actions. Some provide background on the political, social, and economic factors behind a particular decision. Others critique the president's performance, offering a negative or positive appraisal. Essays have been chosen for their concise and engaging presentation of the facts, and each is preceded by a straightforward summary of the article's content.

In addition to the articles, these books include extensive material to help the student researcher. An opening essay provides both a brief biography of the president and an overview of the events that occurred during his time in office. A chronology also helps readers keep track of the dates of specific events. A comprehensive index and an annotated table of contents aid readers in quickly locating material of interest, and an extensive bibliography serves as a launching point for further research. Finally, an appendix of primary historical documents provides a sampling of the president's most important speeches, as well as some of his contemporaries' criticisms.

Greenhaven Press's Presidents and Their Decisions series will help students gain a deeper understanding of the decisions made by some of the most influential leaders in American history.

John F. Kennedy:
A Biography

S HORTLY AFTER NOON ON NOVEMBER 22, 1963, AS THE presidential motorcade traveled through Dallas, Texas, an assassin's bullets mortally wounded President John F. Kennedy. The president was declared dead at 1:00 P.M. at Parkland Hospital in Dallas. Although Lee Harvey Oswald was charged with the murder, Oswald himself was gunned down by Jack Ruby just two days after Kennedy's death. Because Oswald was silenced, questions surrounding the assassination of the president remained unanswered for many, which further added to the myth and intrigue that continues to define Kennedy to the present day.

For Americans living in 1963, the tragic day of Kennedy's death remains etched in their memories, just as it has become part of the national collective conscience. Indeed, it is often said that Kennedy's assassination marked the day America lost its innocence. Few men have been able to capture the national imagination and reflect the hope and ideals of a new generation like the thirty-fifth president. As author Robert Shogun notes, "As powerful as it was during his lifetime, the legend Kennedy wove around his personality took on new vitality after his assassination and left a mark on the presidency that endured long after the abrupt ending of Kennedy's own tenure."[1] Although he lived only forty-six years, Kennedy's legacy endures and looms large over the momentous events surrounding his life and presidency.

Early Years
Rose Fitzgerald Kennedy and Joseph Patrick Kennedy had nine children, the second of which was John Fitzgerald Kennedy, born on May 29, 1917, in Brookline, Massachusetts. John Kennedy (nicknamed "Jack") was born into a

prosperous, political family. He was named after his maternal grandfather, John Francis Fitzgerald, known as "Honey Fitz," the legendary mayor of Boston. The family moved to a larger home during John Kennedy's childhood to accommodate the growing household. In addition to Kennedy's siblings—Joe Jr., Rosemary, Kathleen, Eunice, Patricia, Robert, Jean, and Edward—the bustling, active home was often filled with nannies, housekeepers, and guests.

But it was not always easy for the family. Kennedy's great-grandparents came to the United States from Ireland and encountered anti-Irish and anti-Catholic discrimination. Kennedy's father, Joseph, channeled his negative experiences with discrimination into a drive to succeed, vowing he would make a million dollars while still a young man. His drive and determination were forced on the eldest Kennedy boys by their domineering father, who valued competition and success above all else. This competitive spirit was seen in the touch-football games and other athletic contests played by family members, which were always played to win. As a young boy, Jack also enjoyed swimming, sailing, and other physical activities, and he was encouraged to excel academically as well. The privileges of money allowed Joseph Kennedy to raise his family in Hyannis Port on Cape Cod, Massachusetts; in Palm Beach, Florida; and in other vacation spots for part of each year.

In spite of the robust persona he portrayed in public, Kennedy suffered from countless ailments and illnesses that plagued him through his life. As a child, Jack contracted chicken pox, measles, whooping cough, and scarlet fever, which nearly killed him. Joseph Kennedy even had a priest administer last rites to his young son during this ordeal, convinced the boy would not make it through the illness. Kennedy also suffered from back pain, stemming from an injury while playing football as a schoolboy. Kennedy's bad back, together with his other physical maladies, required him to seek regular care from doctors, who prescribed an alarming array of operations and medications throughout his life. As an adult, Kennedy contracted Addison's disease, which further weakened a man already in severe discomfort and poor health. The family joke was that if Jack were bitten by a mosquito, the mosquito would surely die from Jack's blood.

At age thirteen, Kennedy was sent to study at the Canterbury School in Connecticut, but a bout with appendicitis and other health problems required him to return home before completing his studies. The following year he enrolled in Choate, another prestigious boarding school for boys in Connecticut, graduating in 1935. As a student, Kennedy was active in sports and events and was smart, handsome, and likeable, but his academic performance was only average. However, his budding interest in English,

The Kennedys pose at their Hyannis Port, Massachusetts, summer home in 1948. From left: Jack, Jean, Rose, Joseph, Patricia, Robert, and Eunice; front: Edward (Ted).

writing, and history was formed at Choate. Like his father and older brother, Kennedy went to college at Harvard. Kennedy was never as popular or driven as his older brother Joe Jr., the family's firstborn son, and was far less gregarious and confident. Younger, smaller, and weaker than Joe, Jack regularly received the worst end of their brotherly fights and competition. Joe was always seen by the family—especially by his father—as the child who would make the Kennedys proud and would go into politics.

PT-109

In 1937 Kennedy's father was appointed the U.S. ambassador to England. While the family crossed the Atlantic, the two eldest boys remained stateside at Harvard. During this time, Kennedy was developing an interest in Europe, which was under the fascist threat of Adolf Hitler in Germany and Benito Mussolini in Italy. Hitler's invasion of Poland in 1939 and the start of World War II prompted Kennedy to write his senior thesis on England's unpreparedness for war even in the face of aggression from the fascist powers. It was titled "Appeasement at Munich" and would later be published as the book *Why England Slept*, which earned some notoriety for its young author. Kennedy graduated in 1940.

In 1941 Kennedy joined his older brother in enlisting in the military. During the war Joe Jr. became a pilot in Europe, and Kennedy was a sailor working in naval intelligence in Washington, D.C., and later in the South Pacific. Kennedy gained the rank of lieutenant and in 1943 was given command of *PT-109*, a patrol torpedo boat operating out of the Solomon Islands. It was while on assignment to prevent Japanese ships from resupplying troops that Kennedy had another brush with death and fame. On August 2, 1943, a Japanese destroyer appeared out of nowhere in the dark evening waters, heading full-throttle toward Kennedy's small patrol boat. Lieutenant Kennedy was unable to maneuver quickly enough, and the destroyer sliced the patrol boat in half. Two of the thirteen sailors aboard were unable to escape the carnage and flames and were killed instantly, and Kennedy's bad back was injured in the collision. With their boat sunk, the remaining crew members hung onto floating debris and their injured lieutenant managed to tow a badly burned sailor roughly three miles through the ocean to land by grasping the man's life vest in his teeth.

Ashore on an island, the crew was spotted by islanders who took a coconut shell note carved by Kennedy to nearby British troops. Kennedy and his men were rescued six days later. Kennedy was awarded the Navy and Marine Corps Medal for his bravery, but he had to spend nearly a year at the Chelsea Naval Hospital recovering from the injury to his back and surgery to place a metal plate in his spine.

New Career, New Family

Kennedy's plans for after the war included the possibility of writing or teaching. However, the death of his older brother during the war thrust the second-born son into the role of leading the Kennedy brood. When asked whether he was taking his older brother's place as politician, Kennedy admitted, "No, but I never would have run for office if he had lived. I never would have imagined before the war that I would become active in politics."[2] With his father's encouragement, Kennedy ran for Congress. A new, more disciplined Kennedy invested a lot of hard work and long hours courting voters in Italian and Irish immigrant neighborhoods. In 1946, at the tender age of twenty-eight, John F. Kennedy was elected to represent the Eleventh Congressional District in Massachusetts. The famous Kennedy style was emerging, as he distinguished himself from the "gladhanding" political pros around him. In the words of noted presidential scholar James MacGregor Burns, "[Kennedy] disliked the blarney, the exuberant backslapping and handshaking, the exaggerated claims and denunciations that went with politics."[3]

John F. Kennedy and Jacqueline Lee Bouvier cut their wedding cake after being married on September 12, 1953. Their wedding drew considerable media coverage.

Kennedy was twice reelected to his congressional seat. He then sought a seat in the U.S. Senate in 1952, challenging the well-known incumbent Henry Cabot Lodge. It was an uphill battle, but Kennedy pulled off the upset. As a member of Congress and a war hero, Kennedy was an eligible bachelor in the nation's capital city. Jacqueline ("Jackie") Lee Bouvier, born on July 28, 1929, was, like Kennedy, from a prominent family. With her Miss Porter's finishing school refinement, status as "Debutante of the Year," an education at Vassar and George Washington University, and studies abroad at the Sorbonne in Paris, Bouvier was herself quite a catch. It should thus come as no surprise that their engagement and wedding on September 12, 1953, in Newport, Rhode Island, captured the headlines of the society pages.

With the assistance of his wife, Jackie, and Ted Sorensen, a speechwriter, Kennedy wrote the book *Profiles in Courage*, published in 1956. This study of famous men earned Kennedy the Pulitzer Prize for biography. It also helped launch Kennedy's bid for the vice presidential spot on the 1956 Democratic ticket alongside Adlai Stevenson. But Kennedy was not considered to be an experienced or important legislator by his colleagues in Congress and in the Democratic Party, and he lost the bid.

Life for the young couple was not always easy. Kennedy had additional back operations, nearly dying from one of them, and his wife suffered through a miscarriage and a stillborn daughter. Jacqueline Kennedy, who was by nature sensitive and private, had difficulty getting used to the competitive and aggressive Kennedy family. In addition, the couple was apart a great deal because of Kennedy's political career. Despite these hardships, in 1957 they celebrated the birth of their daughter Caroline.

Presidential Campaign

Events of the late 1950s made possible the campaign of a new type of presidential candidate and the Kennedy campaign. The successful launch by the Soviet Union in 1957 of *Sputnik*, the first satellite in space, shocked the country into the realization that the United States was losing the race for space and possibly the edge in military power. The rising stakes of the Cold War, fears of Chinese aggression, and the French failure to defeat the Communists in Indochina furthered American anxiety. Only miles from Florida, revolutionary Fidel Castro gained power in Cuba in 1958, replacing Fulgencio Batista with a Communist regime. At home, racial unrest coupled with concerns about scientific and technological competition with the Soviets worked against the sitting president, Dwight Eisenhower, who was not in good health and was seen as a passive observer to these momentous events rather than as an engaged leader.

Against this backdrop, Kennedy offered the prospect of change and ran an unconventional campaign. Using the new format of television and harnessing the power of the mass media and film, Kennedy crafted his image as a war hero and courted the public in a manner unseen in previous presidential campaigns. Leading presidential scholars George C. Edwards and Stephen J. Wayne maintain that Kennedy was "a favorite of the press" and the president "exulted in the potential of television for going directly to the people."[4] Perhaps nowhere was this more apparent than in the "Great Debate," the first nationally televised presidential debate between Kennedy and Republican Richard Nixon. The visual image might have provided the important difference in the famous debate, with Kennedy—handsome, comfortable, and personable—gaining the advantage over Nixon—looking pasty and nervous with ill-applied makeup and sweating profusely.

Concerns about Kennedy's youth and Catholicism (Al Smith, who ran as a Democrat in 1928, was the only other Catholic to gain his party's nomination) were deflected by Kennedy's style, charisma, and easy demeanor with the public and press. When asked about his religion, Kennedy was forced to state, "I am not the Catholic candidate for President. I am the Democratic Party's candidate for President, who happens also to be a Catholic."[5] The candidate also reminded his critics, "Nobody asked me if I was a Catholic when I joined the United States Navy and nobody asked my brother if he was a Catholic or a Protestant before he climbed into an American bomber plane to fly his last mission."[6]

Jacqueline Kennedy also proved an asset to the campaign. Attractive, articulate, elegant, and pregnant during the campaign, she also won over crowds, including immigrant communities where she spoke in Italian, Spanish, or French. As in the case of Kennedy's congressional campaigns, the entire family joined the cause: His father, Joe, provided the motivation; his mother, Rose, spoke to community groups; brother Robert ("Bobby") managed the campaign; and Kennedy's sisters hit the campaign trail. Kennedy's confident image, media savvy, and charismatic good looks—honed and effective on the campaign trail—would become hallmarks of his presidency.

The New Frontiers

Kennedy assumed office on November 8, 1960, determined to be an activist and a strong president in the mold of Franklin D. Roosevelt. At forty-three, he was the youngest president ever elected. Kennedy surrounded himself with the brightest minds of his generation and chose for his cabinet a number of very talented and gifted individuals, including Robert McNamara as secretary of defense, McGeorge Bundy as the special assistant for national security, and his own brother, Robert Kennedy, as attorney general. Kennedy hoped to reinvigorate U.S. policies in both foreign affairs and domestic programs and to "get the country moving again."[7] As Kennedy proclaimed in his famous inaugural address, the election of the first president to be born in the twentieth century also signaled the rise of a new generation and a new way of thinking:

> Let the word go forth from this time and place, to friend and foe alike, that the torch has been passed to a new generation of Americans, born in this century, tempered by war, disciplined by a hard and bitter peace, proud of our ancient heritage, and unwilling to witness or permit the slow undoing of those human rights to which this nation has always been committed, and to which we are committed today at home and around the world.[8]

Meanwhile, the Kennedy White House received extensive press coverage. The Kennedys were the first First Family with young children in generations. The family brought a sense of youth to the institution, and Jacqueline Kennedy became a fashion trendsetter. The vigor of the young president and the appeal of the Kennedys led the press to label the White House "Camelot." Kennedy hoped to use his personal popularity to gain congressional approval for his domestic legislative agenda, however, he found himself confronted with a variety of critical foreign policy tests.

Foreign Policy

During the presidential campaign, and then in his inaugural speech, Kennedy rejected calls for a further reduction in tensions with the Soviet Union and instead advocated a renewed commitment to the Cold War struggle. The new president's rhetoric was tested by a succession of international incidents that culminated in the Cuban missile crisis. Throughout these foreign policy crises, Kennedy was determined to counter the increasingly assertive Soviet Union and to bring a sense of optimism and idealism to the foreign affairs of the nation. In other words, he wanted to translate his campaign slogans into policy reality.

Although he realized the importance of countering Soviet aggressiveness, Kennedy genuinely desired to restore U.S. moral leadership as well. Whereas the Eisenhower administration's repeated use of the Central Intelligence Agency (CIA) to undertake covert operations had turned public opinion in many countries against the United States, Kennedy hoped to regain the respect and favor of nations through increased aid and economic assistance. He believed that this tactic would be a less costly and more palatable means to counter Soviet expansion. As a result, many of his foreign policy initiatives were designed to help the average people in developing countries instead of currying favor with the elites through military sales or direct governmental economic aid. Kennedy's initiatives also reflected his belief that the Cold War had been essentially stabilized in Europe and other developed areas of the world, which was a rejection of the Europe-first emphasis of many in the Truman and Eisenhower administrations. Consequently, the new president wanted to craft policies that, according to historian Seyom Brown, reflected his "view that the Third World had now become the decisive field of engagement"[9] for the superpowers.

Almost immediately after he entered office, Kennedy was faced with his first foreign policy test. This incident would reinforce his reluctance to utilize covert operations and reaffirm his preference for nonmilitary competition with the Soviets and their allies. Although the president had hoped that Cuban leader Fidel Castro would emerge as a democratic reformer, by 1961 it was clear that Castro was growing increasingly close with the Soviet Union.

Fidel Castro (shown here with Nikita Khrushchev) assumed control of Cuba in 1959. Kennedy later authorized a covert operation to overthrow Communist Cuba that proved disastrous.

Under the Eisenhower administration, the CIA had drawn up a plan to use Cuban exiles, based in Miami, to overthrow the revolutionary government in Cuba. Kennedy had criticized the previous president for his inactivity on Cuba, yet he did not want to use the American military to overthrow Castro. Hence, the existing CIA plan, with only minimal direct involvement by the United States, seemed a good compromise even though it seemed to violate the spirit of the New Frontier.

The invasion was launched in April 1961 and proved to be a disaster almost from the beginning. Castro's forces put up tougher resistance than the CIA planners had expected. When the U.S.-supported invaders became bogged down on the beaches, Kennedy refused to authorize American military forces to assist them. This led to widespread domestic criticism and caused Soviet leader Nikita Khrushchev to conclude that the American president lacked courage and decisiveness.

Kennedy met with Khrushchev in Vienna in June 1961 in what became a heated and confrontational summit. Khrushchev demanded that the Western countries—France, Great Britain, and the United States—end their occupation of Berlin. The Soviets were concerned that increasing numbers of East Germans were escaping that country's oppressive regime by fleeing into the Allied sectors of Berlin. The Soviet leader even threatened to force the Allied powers to withdraw. The crisis was a reminder that Kennedy could not focus all of his attention on the developing world as events in Europe still had the potential to escalate tensions between the United States and the Soviet Union.

Kennedy refused to be cowed and rejected Khrushchev's demands. He reinforced the U.S. garrison in Berlin and even dispatched Vice President Lyndon B. Johnson to the city to reassure the Germans of the U.S. commitment to the defense of the divided city. Still, Khrushchev's impression of Kennedy continued to be that the new president lacked resolve. For his part, Kennedy became increasingly convinced of the need for strong action to counter Soviet aggression. The Berlin crisis was ultimately only resolved when the Soviets constructed a wall to divide East Berlin from the western sector. Again, the world had avoided a nuclear showdown between the two superpowers, a lesson not lost on Kennedy, who stated, "Now, in the thermonuclear age, any misjudgement on either side about the intentions of the other could rain more devastation in several hours than has been wrought in all the wars of human history."[10]

Foreign Aid Programs

Kennedy recognized the potential for the nation's agricultural surplus to be used as a tool in U.S. foreign policy. During his first days in the White House, Kennedy directed his staff to develop plans that would convert the surplus agricultural harvests of the United States into the basis for food aid. The first result of this effort was the transition of the Agricultural Trade Development and Assistance Act of 1954 (commonly known as Public Law, or PL, 480) in the Food for Peace program. Under Food for Peace, the federal government purchased crops from U.S. farmers and then transferred the foodstuffs to developing nations. This initiative was very popular among the more liberal members of the Democratic Party, including George McGovern and Hubert Humphrey, who wanted to change existing perceptions that U.S. foreign policy was based mainly on military power.

In light of existing tensions with Latin American countries stemming from U.S.-backed covert operations in Guatemala and Cuba, as well as a perception of American economic and political neglect, Kennedy wanted to create a comprehensive policy to increase U.S. aid and attention to the region. The culmination of Kennedy's preferences became known as the Alliance for Progress. Kennedy launched the alliance in a speech on March 13, 1961. Specifically, Kennedy wanted a plan that would accomplish three things over a ten-year period. First, he wanted to reaffirm U.S. support for democracy and project a rejection of previous administrations' support for pro-American dictatorships. Second, Kennedy sought to provide funds for long-term economic development and to stimulate private investment and business interest in the region. The initial plan called for $20 billion in aid over ten years, which would make the alliance larger than the post–World War II Marshall Plan. Finally, the president wanted to expand student exchanges and other cultural interactions between the United States and countries in the region.

The alliance ultimately met with only mixed success. The program was widely popular among most Latin American countries. However, problems in identifying specific programs meant that only about half of the $1.5 billion allocated for the first year was actually disbursed. Many of the individual national assistance programs were plagued by corruption and cost overruns. In addition, the desired increases in private investment failed to materialize. By the end of his presidency, Kennedy faced increasing pressure from both conservatives and liberals in the United States to reform the alliance, and in 1963 Congress significantly decreased funding for the president's aid programs.

The aid program that was closest to Kennedy's heart was the Peace Corps, which the president established through an executive order on March 1, 1961. The young president saw the program as a means to utilize the talents of the "best and brightest" young Americans to spread the values of the United States and to provide aid and assistance to developing countries. The program also proved to be immensely popular with young Americans. The first year of the program, some seven thousand Americans volunteered for the corps, but by 1963 that number had grown to thirty-five thousand. Although the accomplishments of the Peace Corps were not grand since they usually involved individual or small groups of Americans working on local programs, the program continues as one of Kennedy's more enduring legacies.

Vietnam

Although Kennedy wanted to recast U.S.-Soviet superpower competition by expanding American aid programs, he did not hesitate to use military resources as well. Kennedy did not want to repeat the experiences of the Truman administration, which was accused of "losing" China to the Communists. Therefore, the discussions of U.S. policy in Asia became increasingly dominated by proponents of a military solution to Communist-backed revolutions. During the spring and summer of 1961, Kennedy gradually increased the number of American military advisers and special forces troops in Vietnam. Even as the military situation in Vietnam deteriorated through 1962, Kennedy refused to negotiate to end the war.

The continuing inability of U.S. military aid to turn the tide against the Communist Vietcong led Kennedy to begin to recalculate his policy. He began to consider a withdrawal of U.S. forces, however, on November 1, 1963, a coup led to the assassination of Ngo Dinh Diem, the president of South Vietnam, and Kennedy realized that U.S. withdrawal at that point might mean the immediate collapse of the South Vietnamese government. Three weeks later Kennedy would be dead, before any major changes in U.S. policy were implemented.

The Cuban Missile Crisis

The most significant crisis of Kennedy's presidency occurred in October 1962 when U.S. spy planes discovered that the Soviet Union had installed nuclear missile silos in Cuba, just ninety miles from the coast of Florida. Kennedy brought together his closest and brightest advisers into an

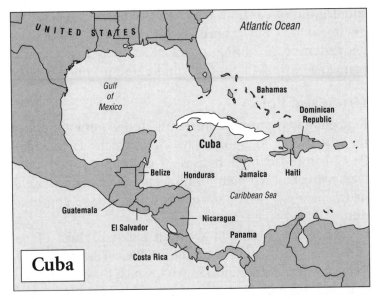

informal body known as EXCOMM (Executive Committee of the National Security Council). The group rejected a diplomatic solution to the crisis and instead devised three possible responses: 1) air strikes to destroy the missile silos; 2) an invasion of the island; or 3) a naval blockade. Kennedy chose the blockade option.

Through careful brinksmanship, Kennedy was able to resolve the crisis without conflict, although the incident marked the closest the world ever came to nuclear war during the Cold War. In Kennedy's words to a nervous nation, he demonstrated both resolve and sensitivity to the grave reality of the situation: "Our goal is not the victory of might but the vindication of right; not peace at the expense of freedom, but both peace and freedom, here in this hemisphere, and, we hope, around the world."[11] Khrushchev ultimately agreed to remove the missiles in exchange for a U.S. pledge to not invade Cuba. The crisis led to the establishment of a telephone "hot line" between Washington and Moscow so that the leaders of the superpowers could in the future negotiate directly before events spiraled out of control. The crisis also led to a general reduction in U.S.-Soviet tensions during the last year of Kennedy's tenure, including the 1963 Test Ban Treaty, which banned atmospheric (but not underground) nuclear tests.

Domestic Policy

Kennedy faced greater constraints in his domestic policy than he did in foreign policy. Although the Democratic Party controlled both houses of Congress, conservative Democrats blocked many of his legislative initiatives. Kennedy's major domestic proposals would not be approved until Johnson's tenure.

Kennedy was able to secure a major package of increased aid for higher education in 1963. That same year, Kennedy signed the Equal Pay Act, which ordered companies with federal contracts to pay men and women equal wages. The president was also able to increase the minimum wage, although the numerous amendments to the legislation limited the impact of the increase. In 1962 Kennedy issued an executive order that banned housing discrimination in developments that were federally funded. All told, in 1961 thirty-three of the fifty-three bills that the administration supported were approved, the following year forty of fifty-four were approved, and in 1963 thirty-five of fifty-eight bills were passed by Congress. This was a better record than the Eisenhower administration, but much of the legislation was minor, and Kennedy was consistently unable to gain approval of his major legislative efforts.

Kennedy sought a significant tax reform program, including reductions in both individual and corporate tax rates. He hoped that the tax changes would stimulate the economy. Congressional opposition to the proposals delayed the legislation for two years. Although the House approved the tax reforms in 1963, the Senate Finance Committee was still holding hearings on the legislation when Kennedy was assassinated.

On February 9, 1961, Kennedy proposed a bill to establish the Medicare health system for the elderly in a special message to Congress. The legislation was introduced into Congress four days later. However, the Senate repeatedly blocked the legislation, and Kennedy was unable to convince southern Democrats to vote in favor of the proposal. By the fall of 1963, writes historian Irving Bernstein, Washington insiders called Medicare "the forgotten issue."[12] It was not until November 1963 that the outlines of an agreement were reached in the Senate Ways and Means Committee. As such, it would fall to the Johnson administration to actually implement the new health care system.

Civil Rights

Civil rights occupied a central place in Kennedy's campaign, and following the election the new president and his closest advisers sought to develop strategies to both strengthen existing civil rights laws and to enact new policies. Kennedy believed that the key to success on civil rights would be to minimize efforts to pass new legislation and instead to maximize the powers of the presidency through executive orders and decisions. Filibusters in the Senate prevented the passage of new laws, so Kennedy sought alternative methods. An early example of this strategy was the November 1962 executive order that forbade discrimination in federal housing. The president also issued Executive Order 10925, which established the Committee on Equal Employment Opportunity to investigate discrimination in hiring and employment practices. Kennedy also directed that the Coast Guard Academy begin admitting African Americans (the first African American entered the academy in 1962).

Kennedy undertook a number of symbolic actions, such as ordering that no members of the administration would attend functions at segregated facilities such as restaurants or hotels. Kennedy also used the federal government's power to regulate interstate commerce to support the Freedom Riders, young activists riding buses through the South in 1961 and 1962 in an attempt to integrate buses and bus terminals. In September 1962 Kennedy dispatched troops from the U.S. Army to quell riots in Oxford, Mississippi, that occurred when James Meredith tried to integrate the University of Mississippi.

Nonetheless, when the administration introduced civil rights legislation in 1962 that focused on voting rights (including the abolition of literacy tests), it encountered opposition and only mounted a halfhearted effort to promote its passage. Kennedy seriously doubted that the legislation would pass the Senate, but he wanted to make a political statement and hoped to use the bill as a means to negotiate less dramatic legislation. Southern senators killed the civil rights measure with a filibuster. By 1963, however, a series of events occurred that led Kennedy to again try to enact a major civil rights bill. In June Kennedy

James Meredith, flanked by U.S. marshals, is escorted onto the University of Mississippi campus in 1962. Kennedy sent U.S. troops to help end segregation there.

had to federalize the Alabama National Guard to integrate the University of Alabama and civil rights leader Medgar Evers was assassinated in Mississippi. In addition, Kennedy wanted the legislation passed so that civil rights would not be an issue in the 1964 presidential election.

On June 19 Kennedy sent to Congress the Civil Rights Act of 1963, which included voting rights provisions, desegregation of public facilities and public education, and new powers for federal agencies to enforce antidiscrimination laws. Once again, southern Democrats and conservatives in the Senate were able to prevent the passage of the bill, even though several attempts were made to craft compromises.

Assassination

As he prepared for the 1964 presidential election, Kennedy could point to a number of successes in foreign policy. The public especially approved of his handling of the Cuban missile crisis. However, he had been unable to secure passage of his major legislative priorities. Still, the young, charismatic president was confident as he began campaigning. He assured voters that his legislative program would be passed within eighteen months.

Tragically, on November 22, 1963, Kennedy was assassinated in Dallas, Texas, while riding in a motorcade. Hence, Americans would never know if Kennedy would have been able to overcome the hurdles he faced in Congress and become a truly great president. Both Kennedy's legacy and the goals he set forth remain as standards by which all subsequent presidents have been judged. In the words of presidential scholar Hugh Davis Graham, "Martyrdom powerfully ennobled the memory of Abraham Lincoln, and its impact on the reputation of the captivating young Kennedy was equally stunning. The world naturally views his presidential legacy through the mythic prism of a Camelot whose hero had fallen."[13]

Kennedy remains a popular president decades after his

death. As presidential scholar James P. Pfiffner notes, "A number of future leaders of both political parties, including President [Bill] Clinton, said that they had been drawn to elected office and public service by Kennedy's inspiring leadership."[14] The ideals Kennedy inspired in his countrymen continue to define the nation: "And so, my fellow Americans, ask not what your country can do for you; ask what you can do for your country. My fellow citizens of the world, ask not what America will do for you, but what together we can do for the freedom of man."[15]

Notes

1. Robert Shogun, *The Double-Edged Sword: How Character Makes and Ruins Presidents: From Washington to Clinton.* Boulder, CO: Westview, 1999, p. 114.

2. Quoted in Arthur M. Schlesinger Jr., *A Thousand Days: John F. Kennedy in the White House.* Greenwich, CT: Fawcett, 1965, pp. 79–89.

3. James MacGregor Burns, *John Kennedy: A Political Profile.* New York: Harcourt Brace, 1959, p. 57.

4. George C. Edwards III and Stephen J. Wayne, *Presidential Leadership: Politics and Policy Making.* 6th ed. Belmont, CA: Wadsworth, 2003, p. 155.

5. Quoted in Robert V. Friedenberg, *Notable Speeches in Comtemporary Presidential Campaigns.* Westport, CT: Praeger, 2002, p. 31.

6. Quoted in Dan B. Fleming Jr., *Kennedy vs. Humphrey, West Virginia, 1960: The Pivotal Battle for the Democratic Presidential Nomination.* Jefferson, NC: McFarland, 1992, p. 33.

7. Quoted in James N. Giglio, *The Presidency of John F. Kennedy.* Lawrence: University Press of Kansas, 1991; or Bruce Miroff, *Icons of Democracy: American Leaders as Heroes, Aristocrats, Dissenters, and Democrats.* New York: McKay, 1993.

8. John F. Kennedy, inaugural address, January 20, 1961.

9. Seyom Brown, *The Faces of Power: United States Foreign Policy from Truman to Clinton.* 2nd ed. New York: Columbia University Press, 1994, pp. 119–20.

10. John F. Kennedy, report to the nation on the Berlin crisis, July 25, 1961.

11. John F. Kennedy, address to the nation on the Cuban missile crisis, November 22, 1962.

12. Irving Bernstein, *Promises Kept: John F. Kennedy's New Frontier.* New York: Oxford University Press, 1991, p. 287.

13. Hugh Davis Graham, "John F. Kennedy," in *The American Presidents.* Ed. Tracy Irons-Georges. Hackensack, NJ: Salem, 2000, p. 568.

14. James P. Pfiffner, *The Modern Presidency.* 3rd ed. Boston: Bedford/St. Martin's, 2000, p. 236.

15. Kennedy, inaugural address.

CHAPTER
1

CONFRONTING
COMMUNISM

Kennedy's Recklessness Led to the Bay of Pigs Invasion

Nancy Gager Clinch

During the presidential campaign of 1960, Kennedy was highly critical of the Eisenhower administration's handling of the Cuban Revolution. Once in office, Kennedy sought to undertake aggressive action to remove Cuba's pro-Soviet leader, Fidel Castro. As a result, Kennedy authorized a CIA operation that involved anti-Castro Cuban exiles in an invasion and attempted overthrow of Castro. Nancy Gager Clinch argues that although Kennedy had misgivings about the covert operation, his personality and his personal heroism led him to authorize the mission. Clinch uses an academic approach known as "psychohistory" to analyze Kennedy's personal qualities as a means to understand his actions. The author was one of the first academics to apply this approach to political biography in the 1970s.

O NLY IN RETROSPECT, AND IN THE PERSPECTIVE OF KEN-nedy's entire Administration, can the psychohistorical meaning of the disastrous Cuban invasion be seen as a logical extension of the general emotional pattern which I have called the "Kennedy neurosis." This recognizable pattern ... appeared to grow out of a deep-seated and unconscious feeling of social and parental rejection suffered by the Kennedy parents and then their children in varying degrees. For the sons, the compensatory defense trends seemed to take the form of a drive toward heroic vindication and virile independence, which was directly tied to an unconscious inner sense of powerlessness. In this context, we can begin to see more clearly how the Bay of Pigs venture appealed to John Kennedy's need for glory and omnipotence and at the same time aroused his secret feelings of helplessness. Irresistible power and immovable powerlessness were the ambivalent dynamics that helped trigger both his rashness in authorizing the invasion and then his inability to closely and rationally supervise the plan. For Kennedy to have supported the feeble invasion with American military force would have compounded the rashness. But not to assure beforehand that the mission had some minimal chance of success, including secrecy, competence, and, above all, a link with the opposition to Castro within Cuba, was an error for which the President as well as his subordinates was responsible. . . .

Escalation

Kennedy's Cuban policy was to some extent the result of his politically expedient responses to Republican charges during the 1960 presidential campaign. In general, Kennedy sought to portray himself as a fighter and man of action, although he also called for the peaceful spread of democratic ideals. But to a considerable degree, Kennedy as President seems to have become a victim of his own extreme campaign oratory. From early October, 1960, candidate Kennedy had hammered ceaselessly on the theme that Cuba had become "communism's first Caribbean base" because of Republican blunders. Vice President Nixon retorted by calling (on October 18) for a quarantine of Cuba, and Eisenhower backed him up the next day with a sweeping trade embargo. Senator Kennedy sharply criticized the embargo as "too little and too late" after "an incredible history of blunder, inaction, retreat and failure." Said Kennedy, "For six years before Castro came to power the Republicans did absolutely nothing to stop the rise of communism in Cuba. Our Ambassadors repeatedly warned the Republicans of mounting danger. But the warning was ignored...." The Democratic candidate urged stronger sanctions and an American effort "to strengthen the non-Batista Democratic forces in exile and in Cuba itself...." Nixon struck back by accusing Kennedy of advocating a "shockingly reckless" proposal that would be "a direct invitation for the Soviet Union to intervene militarily on the side of Cuba." (It later came to light that Nixon at that time was privately approving the CIA support of anti-Castro groups in Miami.)

In the October 21 television "debate" between Kennedy and Nixon, the two Cold Warrior candidates . . . jousted over Cuba in words that two veteran reporters . . . called "the campaign's low in political humbug." By then, Castro had nationalized the Cuban sugar industry, and invasion rumors grew to the point where the Cuban delegation to the United Nations in November brought a formal charge of such planning against the United States. In fact, President Eisenhower had directed the CIA to recruit and train Cuban exiles as early as March 17, 1960, although at that time only guerrilla action was contemplated. But such projects have an inner momentum, and the CIA plan grew steadily in size and irrationality. From the initial concept of small groups slipping into Cuba to form centers of resistance, the idea grew to include a direct beachhead assault in multiple landings. Kennedy, however, knew nothing of this project until after his election, when CIA chief Allen Dulles briefed him on November 17, 1960. Kennedy decided to continue the project, but as an option rather than as a definite decision. At that time the President-elect was too busy forming his new Administration to think much about Cuba. Thus the CIA went ahead in its secret planning and training of the Cubans in Guatemala. In December, the multiple-landings strategy evolved into a single invasion force which would hold a beachhead long enough to attract activists and defectors from Castro and set off a general uprising. Later the idea was added that an exile government would be flown in which could then call for U.S. support. In case of failure, the invaders could retreat to the mountains. But the ground rule held: no American forces would participate in the initial invasion. The CIA hoped to repeat its 1954 Guatemala coup, although it conveniently overlooked the vastly different conditions in Cuba.

The Plan

In January 1961, as Kennedy took office, the Joint Chiefs of Staff [JCS] for the first time began to consider possible levels of U.S. military involvement in the CIA plan. Meanwhile, recruitment of Cuban exiles was stepped up, and the CIA consolidated its control of the invasion leadership. Castro could follow almost every detail of these machinations, for CIA and Cuban security was unbelievably lax—and Castro's agents were everywhere among the politically divergent groups in Florida. Equally crucial, the initial inclusion of the Cuban underground in the planning was largely dropped. On January 22, leading Kennedy advisers, including Secretary of State Rusk, Defense Secretary McNamara, and Robert Kennedy, reviewed the plan. On January 28, President Kennedy held his first White House review. [Kennedy adviser Arthur] Schlesinger described Kennedy as "wary and reserved in his reaction." The President ordered Defense to review the CIA military plans and the State Department to prepare a program for isolating Cuba through the Organization of American States (OAS). Overt U.S. participation in an invasion was still ruled out. The JCS produced an ambiguous evaluation, but finally concluded in early March that internal resistance was indispensable to success.

Other events combined to confront Kennedy with what Schlesinger called "a now-or-never choice" in mid-March: Guatemala asked for the departure of the invasion force from its soil by the end of April; the Cuban fighters were demanding action and they might be demoralized by further postponement; the rainy season would soon begin; and, perhaps most pressing, Castro would shortly receive jet airplanes from Russia and Cuban pilots trained in Czechoslovakia. According to Schlesinger, "After June 1, it would take the United States Marines and Air Force to overthrow Castro. If a purely Cuban invasion were ever to take place, it had to take place in the next few weeks." All at once, it seemed, Kennedy's presumed planning contingency had turned into an urgent reality. . . .

Fifty-Fifty Chance

In the face of such forcefully presented arguments, "Kennedy tentatively agreed that the simplest thing, after all, might be to let the Cubans go where they yearned to go—to Cuba." But he was very concerned about the political risk, and wanted a quiet night landing. Again, Kennedy insisted there would be no U.S. military intervention. No one at the time objected, although in the light of events it seems clear that many people both inside and outside the government expected Kennedy to intervene if necessary. *New York Times* editor Herbert Matthews, for example, assumed that, if necessary, Kennedy would support the invasion with American force, using anti-Communist arguments to justify the intervention. Reportedly Kennedy told a *Times* editor the day before the landing that he thought the invasion had a "fifty-fifty chance." One can only wonder what contradictory feelings of success and failure were passing through the President at this time.

Kennedy and his counsellors met again on March 15, when "the President, listening somberly, suggested some changes, mostly intended to 'reduce the noise level'—such as making sure that the invasion ships would be unloaded before dawn." Then Kennedy authorized the planners to proceed, but in a way that would allow him to call off the invasion as late as twenty-four hours ahead. Kennedy also repeated his decision against any form of U.S. military intervention. (As it turned out, the first frogmen ashore were Americans; and at least four Americans were killed piloting B-26's over Cuba. Also when defeat loomed, Kennedy allowed a two-hour fighter cover from nearby carriers, but because of a mix-up the jets arrived too late to save the B-26's. Thus some overt intervention did occur, although it was petty compared with the overriding fact that the United States had planned, directed, organized, financed, and transported the entire operation.) At this March 15 meeting, Kennedy stated that he was still reserving final judgment. . . .

Wishful Thinking?

Both Kennedy and his advisers suffered from a neurotic form of wishful thinking that was to lead them from the deadly swamps of Cuba to the rice-paddy quagmire of Vietnam. The euphoria of the Kennedy Administration after Kennedy's astonishing winning of the presidency was evident to Schlesinger, who in many ways was the most realistic and candid of the Kennedy counsellors (but, unfortunately, one of the least influential). . . . In discussing the President's final decision to go ahead, Schlesinger noted Kennedy's "enormous confidence in his own luck. . . . Everything had broken right for him since 1956. . . . Everyone around him thought he had the Midas touch and could not lose. Despite himself, even this dispassionate and skeptical man may have been affected by the soaring euphoria of the new day."

In truth, Kennedy was not nearly as "dispassionate" and "skeptical" as his eulogizers have portrayed him. The Kennedy sons frequently exhibited a strong sense of personal luck, intermingled with a fatalistic feeling of personal doom. JFK fully shared this emotional duality. From the psychological view, a belief in either luck or fatalism is often a rationalization for darker, unconscious influences at work in one's personality. Indeed, Kennedy's confidence, while sometimes warranted by careful planning (as in his campaigns), led him to take extraordinary risks and deal in illusions uncorrected by hard questions and close study (as, again, exemplified by Cuba and Vietnam). In the international realm, where Kennedy's hopes of glory essentially lay, his deep caution and skepticism led him to take superficial safeguards; but again and again, his deeply repressed contradictory drive toward neurotic self-glorification and self-defeat seemed to be stronger.

Thus, in the spring of 1961, the important questions that would have dissolved the veil of illusion which Kennedy and his top advisers had woven for themselves remained too little asked and too little answered. Kennedy still had serious reservations, but he had been misled into believing that the operation had been coordinated with the Cuban underground. In fact, the CIA intended to invade without depending on sabotage and insurrection from within. It was one of several crucial mistakes, for Castro's men temporarily imprisoned almost the entire underground among the 200,000 suspects they arrested.

Advice and Action

In the light of what we know today, the intelligence failures of Kennedy's responsible advisers in this episode are quite extraordinary. Schlesinger reported in his history that British Ambassador David Ormsby Gore later told him that British intelligence estimates, which had been given to the CIA, "showed that the Cuban people were still predominantly behind Castro and there was no likelihood at this point of mass defections or insurrections." A 1969 study of U.S. interventions, *By Weight of Arms: America's Overseas Military Policy*, confirmed that this fact was well known even outside the military and intelligence establishment. As the authors noted, "The primary cause of the failure was the lack of popular support in Cuba, the key assumption in

Kennedy's Personality

Author and columnist Richard Reeves discusses Kennedy's beliefs and decision-making style.

Kennedy was decisive, though he never made a decision until he had to, and then invariably he chose the most moderate of available options. His most consistent mistake in governing, as opposed to politics, was thinking that power could be hoarded for use at the right moment—but moments and conditions defied reason. He had little ideology beyond anti-Communism and faith in active, pragmatic government. And he had less emotion. What he had was an attitude, a way of taking on the world, substituting intelligence for ideas or idealism, questions for answers. What convictions he did have, on nuclear proliferation or civil rights or the use of military power, he was often willing to suspend, particularly if that avoided confrontation with Congress or the risk of being called soft. If some would call that cynicism, he would see it as irony. "Life is unfair," he said, in the way the French said, *C'est la vie.* Irony was as close as he came to a view of life: things are never what they seem.

"No one ever knew John Kennedy, not all of him," said Charlie Bartlett.

That was obviously the way Kennedy wanted it. All his relationships were bilateral. He was a compartmentalized man with much to hide, comfortable with secrets and lies. He needed them because that was part of the stimulation: things *were* rarely what they seemed. He called people when he wanted them, for what he wanted then. His children came at the clap of his hands and were swooped up and taken away at a nod to a nanny. After his election, he said his the planning of the invasion. The Cuban people, especially the peasantry, which comprised most of the population, were thoroughly satisfied with the Castro regime.". . . But as

---

White House organization would look like a wheel with many spokes and himself at what he called "the vital center."

"It was instinctive at first," he said. "I had different identities, and this was a useful way of expressing each without compromising the others."

There was an astonishing density of event during the Kennedy years. In October of 1962, the President was still grappling with the riots that began with the admission of the first Negro to the University of Mississippi when he was shown the aerial photographs that proved the Soviets were putting nuclear missiles into Cuba. In one forty-eight-hour period in June 1963, he gave the speech of his life trying to break the world's nuclear siege, America was changed by a church bombing in Alabama, and the world was changed by a monk burning himself to death on a street in Saigon. On an August day when more than two hundred thousand Americans were marching for civil rights in Washington, Kennedy was giving the orders that led to the assassination of an annoying ally, the president of South Vietnam.

John F. Kennedy was one of only forty-two men who truly knew what it is like to be President. He was not prepared for it, but I doubt that anyone ever was or will be. The job is sui generis. The presidency is an act of faith.

On the morning after the new President's first night in the White House, Charlie Bartlett asked him if he had slept in Abraham Lincoln's bed, and Kennedy answered that he had: "I jumped in and just hung on!" He was still hanging on three years later.

Richard Reeves, *President Kennedy: Profile of Power*. New York: Simon & Schuster, 1993, pp. 19–20.

Schlesinger makes clear, the top proponents of the invasion, such as CIA chiefs Allen Dulles and Richard Bissell, did not ask for assessments from their subordinates (who might be expected to know what outside experts, such as sociologists, were thinking). . . . The entire invasion was predicated on an internal uprising, for the military force involved was vastly inferior to Castro's armed strength. While it is true that Kennedy was greatly misguided by his intelligence men, this does not exonerate the President from a personal naiveté and romantic wishful thinking in two areas where he had direct experience, war and politics—a naiveté, we might note, that was not shared by a mere history professor, Arthur Schlesinger, Jr. (Kennedy was also supposed to be a historian of some stature.)

The White House meetings continued through March with little opposition. The strongest objector to the invasion was Senator William Fulbright, chairman of the Senate Foreign Relations Committee. He wrote Kennedy to argue against the forceful overthrow of Castro, saying that such a policy would violate the OAS charter, hemisphere treaties, and U.S. legislation. If the invasion succeeded, it "would be denounced from the Rio Grande to Patagonia as an example of imperialism." If we used our own arms, the United States "would have undone the work of thirty years in trying to live down earlier interventions." And we might be left with an onerous responsibility for post-Castro Cuba. "To give this activity even covert support," wrote Fulbright, "is of a piece with the hypocrisy and cynicism for which the United States is constantly denouncing the Soviet Union in the United Nations and elsewhere. This point will not be lost on the rest of the world—nor on our own consciences." Fulbright urged containment instead through the Alliance for Progress. . . .

Whatever the exact source of John F. Kennedy's new determination, the climactic meeting took place on April 4 after his return. The President asked each adviser in turn to give his opinion. Only Fulbright denounced the operation as, according to Schlesinger, "wildly out of proportion to the threat. It would compromise our moral position in the world and make it impossible for us to protest treaty violations by the Communists."... As the Harvard historian logically pointed out, "No matter how 'Cuban' the equipment and personnel, the U.S. will be held accountable for the operation, and our prestige will be committed to its success." Secondly, since evidence for a mass insurrection was lacking, the operation might turn into a prolonged civil conflict that would bring strong political pressure on Kennedy to intervene. What was lacking was a direct and demonstrable threat to U.S. security. Without it, such an action could only seem like a "calculated aggression" to much of the world. Schlesinger feared that an invasion would destroy the international credibility of Kennedy himself, which he saw as one of America's greatest assets. . . .

Consequences

Schlesinger generally supports this impression that Kennedy was a prisoner of basic misconceptions as well as momentum. By Saturday, April 8, the President seemed to have made up his mind. According to Schlesinger, Kennedy said he had successfully reduced the operation "from a grandiose amphibious assault to a mass infiltration." The President accepted CIA assurances about the contingency escape and felt that failure, if it came, could now be tolerated. "If we have to get rid of these 800 men," JFK told Schlesinger, "it is much better to dump them in Cuba than in the United States, especially if that is where they want to go." The historian felt that Kennedy's decision also resulted from his newness in office, and believed that the opposition of one senior adviser would have led to cancellation. . . .

Yet Sorensen has sharply criticized Kennedy's handling of the Bay of Pigs incident, and his comments are psychologically significant. According to Sorensen, the President made "many and serious" mistakes. The President should have had, despite his recent arrival in the Oval Office, the confidence to cancel the plans of the experts and the exiles, but he did not because he feared he would be thought arrogant and presumptuous. Kennedy should have known his advisers better and should never have proceeded, so early in his Administration, with a project about which he had deep misgivings. Sorensen's litany continues: Kennedy let his deep personal antipathy to Castro interfere with his better judgment; he was overconcerned with public opinion and what the reaction might be if it was learned that he had abandoned a plan to dispose of Castro; he should have moved the brigade from Guatemala to another camp and given more thought to its future; and if he had disbanded the brigade, the consequences would have been milder than the course he chose. . . .

There is no need to go into the military details of the Bay of Pigs catastrophe. Two days before the landing, Cuban-piloted B-26's made dawn attacks in an unsuccessful attempt to destroy Castro's air force. The raid's results were exaggerated to Kennedy, and as a result he cancelled a second strike. The effects of this cancellation were later vastly distorted by the press; in reality, the second raid, even if successful, could only have postponed the Brigade's defeat. The clumsy CIA plot, which included the wrong type of B-26's as alleged Cuban planes seized by defectors, merely alerted Castro further. Even worse, it severely embarrassed Adlai Stevenson, the U.S. Ambassador to the U.N., who had not been informed of this secret plan and publicly claimed American innocence. The entire invasion was carried out with this same ill-fated lack of care and overoptimistic bungling. In addition, Castro and his forces were unexpectedly efficient and well organized. There was no revolt in the 250,000-member Cuban army and militia; Castro's patrols and planes reacted vigorously; his soldiers fought hard, while his police rounded up potential resisters; and Castro himself led his forces with skill. The Cuban Brigade landed in the early hours of Monday, April 17; on Wednesday they were forced to surrender to overwhelming forces.

Lessons Learned

Kennedy himself took the stunning fiasco with outer calm, for he was a man of great composure in times of crisis. Emotional detachment, . . . was one of Kennedy's chief psychological defenses, and in defeat it could be a useful protection. Yet while Kennedy assumed full public responsibility for the Bay of Pigs, he also subtly disclosed to friends among the press some of the inside story, an indirect way of sharing blame. In addition, his White House staff held "backgrounders" for the press which revealed CIA and JCS ineptitudes. Schlesinger recounts that on that tragic Wednesday, the President invited him and James Reston, *The New York Times* Washington Bureau Chief, to lunch. "In spite of the news, Kennedy was free, calm and candid; I had rarely seen him more effectively in control. Saying frankly that reports from the beaches were discouraging, he spoke with detachment about the problems he would now face. 'I probably made a mistake in keeping Allen Dulles on,' he said. 'It's not that Dulles is not a man of great ability. He is. But I have never worked with him, and therefore I can't estimate his meaning when he tells me things. . . . Dulles is a legendary figure, and it's hard to operate with legendary figures. . . . It is a hell of a way to learn things, but I have learned one thing from this business— that is, that we will have to deal with CIA.'". . .

Another aide later disclosed Kennedy's unpublicized reaction: "When it happened, the President was hit hard. He showed his fatigue for the first time. He looked sad. The exhilaration of the job was gone. He was no longer the young conquering hero, the first forty-three-year-old president, the first Catholic president, the young man smoking his cigar with his friends and telling them how much fun it was. All that was gone. Suddenly it became one hell of a job."

On April 20, a day after the surrender, Kennedy delivered a scheduled speech before the American Society of Newspaper Editors in Washington. . . . The President's address was a rather typical example of obscure but vigorous Kennedy rhetoric; it made him appear as a fighter without committing him to any specific action. "Let the record show," he stated, "that our restraint is not inexhaustible. Should it ever appear that the inter-American doctrine of non-interference merely conceals or excuses a policy of non-action—if the nations of the Hemisphere should fail to meet their commitments against outside Communist penetration—then I want it clearly understood that the Government will not hesitate in meeting its primary obligations which are to the security of our Nation.". . .

Richard J. Walton, in his insightful interpretation of Kennedy's foreign policies, *Cold War and Counterrevolution*, points out how Kennedy's apologists claimed that JFK learned a valuable lesson from the Bay of Pigs. Walton shows the falseness of this claim, for if we are to judge by the evidence, Kennedy and his advisers learned nothing. The Cuban invasion led eventually to the missile crisis, when Khrushchev recklessly tried to protect his protégé from further invasion, and before that the Kennedy Administration approached the brink in Berlin and edged into Vietnam.

But Walton also unequivocally states the deeper meaning of the Bay of Pigs, a lesson which is the underlying meaning of emotional neurotic conflict: the inevitable link between irrationality and immorality. Neurosis is a human sickness which prevents the victim from achieving his own humanity and thus from fulfilling his capacity for ethical living. The result, in the case of Kennedy and his advisers, was the passion for power and intellectual arrogance which brought about the inhumanities of such militaristic "adventures." As Walton wisely wrote, "Although it seemed a transient episode during Kennedy's administration, the Bay of Pigs was profoundly revealing. It demonstrated that Kennedy, like his predecessors, like his society, was excessively preoccupied with communism, that he was an interventionist prepared to violate national sovereignty in an attempt to strike it down. It demonstrated that Kennedy lacked prudence, an essential quality in the nuclear age. . . . But even if the planning had not been an exercise in gross incompetence, even if it had not demonstrated a profound ignorance of revolution, even if it had not revealed a political attitude that would lead to more dangerous adventures, even if it had not led directly to the Cuban missile crisis, the Bay of Pigs would have still left an indelible stain on Kennedy's record. It was wrong."

The Berlin Crisis Set the Tone for Kennedy's Policy Toward the Soviets

Seyom Brown

The status of Berlin was a source of tension between the United States and the Soviet Union until the end of the Cold War. In 1945, Berlin was divided into four zones, each under the control of one of the four main Allied powers—Great Britain, France, the Soviet Union, and the United States. In 1961, the Soviets attempted to force the Western allies to permanently recognize the division of Berlin, which would mean the official recognition of Soviet control of East Germany.

Seyom Brown, a professor at Brandeis University, discusses how the Berlin crisis strengthened Kennedy's view that the United States needed to be strong in the face of Soviet aggression, while also avoiding war. In a July 25, 1961, address, Kennedy vowed that the United States and its allies would fight to keep West Berlin non-Communist. When the Soviets sealed East Berlin and erected the Berlin Wall to divide the city, the United States made largely symbolic statements but stopped short of provoking the Soviets. The tension surrounding the Berlin crisis set the tone for future U.S.-Soviet confrontations.

Seyom Brown, *The Faces of Power: United States Foreign Policy from Truman to Clinton*. New York: Columbia University Press, 1994. Copyright © 1994 by Columbia University Press. All rights reserved. Reproduced by permission.

O N THE ISSUES OF BERLIN AND THE MISSILES IN CUBA President Kennedy displayed most clearly his appreciation of the central function played by military power as an arbiter of conflicting goals and wills in international relations. These two crises also indicated the gap between the reality of a bipolar organization of effective power in the international system and the hope for a pluralistic world based on self-determination. Berlin and Cuba compelled Kennedy, at least temporarily to renew the bipolar basis for coping with the fierce conflicts in a world armed with nuclear power and without a central system of law and order. He could still hope that such a two-sided balance of power, sustained by each superpower's fear of the other's military prowess, could become the basis for a more peaceful phase of competition between the Communists and non-Communists. A period of peaceful competition based on well-defined and mutually respected spheres of control, might eventually lead to depreciation of military power as the currency behind most international transactions, and to a less rigid international order.

The few United States official statements on Berlin in early 1961 conveyed a stiffer posture on Berlin and Germany than had been displayed by the Eisenhower administration during the previous round of negotiations in 1959. In the city, on March 8, 1961, Averell Harriman, the President's roving ambassador explicitly disassociated the new administration from the Eisenhower administration's concessionary proposals. "All discussions on Berlin," he said, "must begin from the start." At the same time Kennedy, through Ambassador Llewellyn Thompson, sent a personal note to Premier Khrushchev suggesting a meeting between the two leaders to clear the air—not for purposes of negotiation, but rather for each side to better understand the other's basic commitments so as to remove any chance of miscalculations that might lead to war.

At the Vienna Summit (June 3–5, 1961), the Soviet

Premier was very tough on Berlin, using language close to the tone of an ultimatum: a peace treaty recognizing East German jurisdiction over access to Berlin would be signed in December and wartime occupation rights would be ended. If the West tried to violate the sovereign rights of the Ulbricht regime, force would be met with force. It was up to the United States to choose whether there would be war or peace. At the close of their talks, Kennedy was handed an official Soviet *aide-mémoire*, somewhat less belligerent in tone, but clearly heralding a resumption of the Berlin conflict. . . .

The Soviet Position

The Soviets were proposing, in short, an agreement to legitimize the division of Germany, with East Berlin under the complete authority of the Ulbricht regime and West Berlin an international city. The Soviets and their allies would be given as much control over the Administration of West Berlin as the United States and its allies. Access to this international city—located within East Germany—would be controlled by the East German government. Agreement would have been to capitulate to the essence of the demands Khrushchev had been making with respect to Germany since 1958. Why was Khrushchev renewing these demands with such vigor and confidence now? This question bothered President Kennedy and his associates in their post mortems on the Vienna conference. Were the Soviets emboldened by perceptions that the strategic nuclear balance was such as to make Communist local military superiority in Central Europe the only relevant factor of power? Had the Bay of Pigs adventure and Kennedy's backing away from a superpower showdown over Laos given Khrushchev the impression that the United States would be the first to swerve off a collision course? The President, in his discussions with the Soviet Premier at Vienna, may have sensed that Khrushchev might underestimate the Kennedy resolve and nerve under pressure. Kennedy was careful to choose the words and demeanor to disabuse him of such notions. Sorensen and Schlesinger both recount Kennedy's response to Khrushchev's insistence that the decision to change the occupation status of West Berlin by December was irrevocable, whether the United States agreed or not. If that was the case, retorted the President, "it will be a cold winter."

The U.S. Position

The President's instincts were to open up the Berlin issue to a wide set of alternatives, and for the United States to set the terms of reference, rather than always reacting to Soviet proposals. But he was unwilling to enter into negotiations with only the increasingly unbelievable "trip wire" military posture in Western Europe to back him up. Accordingly, he put his foreign policy advisers, including elder statesman Acheson, to work on developing an expanded list of political options while he put the Defense Department to work on increasing his military options.

His advisers found it easier to be creative when proposing military measures than when proposing political approaches. The State Department, designed more to implement and reiterate established policy premises than to generate new ones, responded characteristically; it took exasperatingly long, but it came up eventually with a statement of the U.S. position on Berlin which turned out to be little more than a marginally updated amalgam of positions developed in the 1950s. Acheson's proposals had more substance but were also designed primarily for strengthening the U.S. hand in the status quo, rather than changing the status quo. Backed by Vice President Johnson, Acheson urged a presidential proclamation of national emergency accompanied by an immediate expansion of military manpower, including the calling up of reserves, a $5 billion increase in the defense budget, plus new taxation and standby controls on wages and prices. Openly preparing the nation for the worst and visibly making the economy ready for war would demonstrate to Khrushchev, more starkly than any manipulation of U.S. military capabilities in the vicinity of Berlin, that current Soviet threats were merely stimulating the U.S. to enhance its commitments and to more thoroughly involve the national honor in those commitments. . . .

Kennedy Acts

Kennedy rejected the suggestion for an immediate declaration of national emergency, but incorporated some of the major premises underlying the Acheson proposals into his own planning. He knew that words were not enough to dissuade the Soviets. The military increase that the President had already ordered as part of his program for remedying the nation's military deficiencies would be accelerated under the impetus of the Berlin crisis to convince Khrushchev that his bluster could lead only to the firming up of U.S. resolve. The President did not unequivocally reject the more extreme suggestions of a large-scale mobilization and a declaration of national emergency. These might yet have to be used; but not so early in the crisis. The grand strategy should be the classical one of arming to parley; the U.S. *wanted* the parley, in an atmosphere conducive to calm deliberation on terribly complicated conflicts of interest. Showdowns could only revive the simplifications of the cold war, and possibly lead to hot war.

The President's television address on July 25 was designed to be both very tough and more reasonable than previous United States statements on the Berlin issue. The non-Communist presence in West Berlin, and access thereto, could not be ended by any act of the Soviet government, the President told the world. It would be a mistake to consider Berlin, because of its location, as a tempting target: "I hear it said that West Berlin is militarily untenable. And so was Bastogne. And so, in fact, was Stalingrad. Any dangerous spot is tenable if men—brave men—will make it so." The city had become "the greatest testing place of Western courage and will, a focal point where our solemn commitments . . . and Soviet ambitions now meet in basic confrontation." Berlin was no less protected than the rest of the West, "for we cannot separate its safety from our own."

He warned the Soviets not to make the dangerous but common mistake of assuming that the West was too soft, too divided in the pursuit of narrow national interests, to fight to preserve its objectives in Berlin. Too much was at

In 1961 President Kennedy met with Nikita Khrushchev in Vienna, Austria, to determine the fate of West Berlin. Kennedy resolved to keep West Berlin free.

stake for the alliance as a whole: "For the fulfillment of our pledge to that city is essential to the morale and security of Western Germany, to the unity of Western Europe, and the faith of the entire Free World . . . in . . . our willingness to meet our commitments."

Accordingly, in addition to the supplementary defense buildup the President had asked the Congress to approve in March, he was now asking for $3.25 billion more—most of it to be spent on the capability-in-being to deploy rapidly to the Central European front without weakening the U.S. ability to meet commitments elsewhere. The measures included a tripling of the draft calls for the coming months, the ordering up of certain reserve and National Guard units, the reactivation of many deactivated planes and ships, and a major acceleration in the procurement of nonnuclear weapons.

The President wanted to make it clear that "while we will not let panic shape our policy," he was contemplating still more dramatic steps if the situation required them. . . .

Showdown

Khrushchev, discussing disarmament issues with John J. McCloy, told McCloy in emotional tones that he was angered by the President's speech and professed to find in it only an ultimatum akin to a preliminary declaration of war.

By this time, however, the flow of refugees from East Berlin to West Berlin was seriously damaging Soviet prestige and the manpower resources of East Germany. Khrushchev may have welcomed an atmosphere of imminent explosion as the context for his sealing of the boundary between East and West Berlin just three weeks after the Kennedy address.

On August 7, the Soviet Premier delivered one of the most belligerent speeches of his career, linking "military hysteria" in the United States with an "orgy of revanchist passions" in West Germany, and warning the West against any intervention under the illusion that there could be a limited war over Berlin. Khrushchev, bestowing honors on Cosmonaut Titov, used the occasion to make pointed allusions to the strategic power of the Soviet Union. "Any states used as a springboard for an attack upon the Socialist camp will experience the full devastating power of our blow." The territory of the United States would be crushed. Intervention, an act of war by the West, would be a suicidal act, spelling "death to millions upon millions of people."

When East Berlin was sealed six days later, the specter of thermonuclear holocaust had already been projected. The next move was up to the United States. The U.S. could accept the Soviet claim of acting to stabilize and bottle up the combustible passions on both sides of the boundary to within controllable confines. Or the U.S. could define it as a unilateral abrogation of established four-power responsibility for the city as a whole and a shameless denial of free choice to the Berliners, thus placing it into that category of action the President insisted had to be resisted. Khrushchev was gambling on the vividness of the nuclear backdrop as the main barrier to Western action. The "wall" at first consisted of double strands of barbed wire and other light barricades, backed up by elements of a motorized division of the East German Army at critical crossing points. Western counteraction could have taken the form of a symbolic cutting of the wire, or pushing over of some obstacles. It need not have involved anything as dramatic as a bull-dozing operation with tanks and cannon; and the next move would have been up to the Soviets. Khrushchev still had many options. His gamble, of course, was that the West would not "overreact."

The Soviets launched a well-planned diplomatic campaign, calculated to provide the Western nations with a convincing political excuse for doing nothing. On August 13, the Warsaw Pact countries issued a declaration against "subversive activities directed from West Berlin" against the "socialist countries." The pact members accordingly requested the East Germans

> to establish an order on the borders of West Berlin which will securely block the way to the subversive activity . . . so that reliable safeguards and effective control can be established around the whole territory of West Berlin, including its border with democratic Berlin. . . .

Kennedy sought advice from advisers at home and abroad, and found a solid consensus that there was not much he could do apart from issuing verbal protests. Sorensen recounts that "not one responsible official in the country, in West Berlin, West Germany, or Western Europe—suggested that allied forces should march into East German territory and tear the Wall down." The mayor of Berlin, Willy Brandt, in a personal letter to President Kennedy, demanded retaliatory actions such as a selective ban on imports from East Germany, a refusal to issue travel permits to East German officials, and the takeover of the portion of the elevated railroad system in West Berlin that was still administered by the East. He also called for special actions to demonstrate renewed support by the United States for the West Berliners, many of whom felt that the West's failure to prevent the erection of the wall meant that the balance had been tipped in the Soviets' favor and it was only a matter of time before the noose was tightened around the entire city. From the symbolic actions suggested by Brandt, four were adopted by the White House during the next few days.

- the reinforcement of the allied garrison in West Berlin;
- the appointment of General Lucius Clay as the American commandant;
- the movement of allied troops along the Autobahn into West Berlin to demonstrate the continuing rights of Western access;
- the dispatch of Vice President Johnson to the city.

The Wall

The wall remained and was reinforced with bricks and mortar. In a number of incidents refugees trying to escape were brutally mistreated. A confrontation between Soviet and American tanks across the barriers was among the rather daring demonstrations of resolve by General Clay. West Berlin remained Western and the allies continued to exercise their rights of access to the city while refusing to grant recognition to the East German regime. December 1961 came and went and the Soviets refrained from carrying out the unilateral actions threatened in their July *aide-mémoire*. . . .

Berlin and the other diplomatic crises of Kennedy's first year could be viewed as tests of the ground rules for coexistence that the President propounded to Khrushchev during their conversations in Vienna no action by either superpower to alter the existing balance of power and no attempt by either to interfere within the other's sphere of control. At Vienna there seemed to be mutual agreement to these ground rules in principle, but considerable differences over how they might apply in practice: there was no objective definition of the balance of power, nor could the President and the Chairman assent unequivocally to the other's definition of legitimate spheres of control. The Berlin conflict was the product of these differences, not the cause. Neither side could agree simply to a maintenance of the "status quo." Moreover, with so many new nations experimenting with various types of regimes and still determining their international interests and inclinations, there was not even a de facto status quo in the Third World. Consequently a series of tests in a volatile environment would determine who had effective power over what, and where, at any one time, the spheres of control lay.

Kennedy Handled the Cuban Missile Crisis Effectively

William H. Kautt

In October 1962 the Kennedy administration discovered that the Soviet Union was installing medium-range nuclear missiles in Cuba, ninety miles from U.S. shores. This discovery initiated a tense standoff between Kennedy and Soviet leader Nikita S. Khrushchev that lasted nearly two weeks. In the end, the Soviets agreed to remove the weapons from Cuba in exchange for Kennedy's assurance that he would remove missiles from Turkey that were aimed at the Soviet Union.

In the following selection, William H. Kautt argues that Kennedy handled the crisis well. By relying on negotiations rather than force, Kennedy averted a nuclear war and created a precedent for future cooperation between the two superpowers. Kautt is a captain in the U.S. Air Force and a former assistant professor of history at the U.S. Air Force Academy in Colorado.

THE CUBAN MISSILE CRISIS (OCTOBER 1962) BEGAN WHEN U.S. military reconnaissance flights provided proof that the Soviets were placing medium-range nuclear missiles in Cuba, ninety miles from Florida. This move was a destabilizing one as it reduced dramatically the flight time of, and hence the reaction time to, nuclear missiles that might be

William H. Kautt, *History in Dispute, Volume 6, The Cold War: Second Series*, edited by Dennis E. Showalter and Paul DuQuenoy. Detroit: St. James Press, 2000. Copyright © 2000 by St. James Press. Reproduced by permission of The Gale Group.

used to attack the United States. The United States was not friendly with Cuba, and the possibility of a communist regime in the Western Hemisphere possessing nuclear weapons was unacceptable. President John F. Kennedy decided to assert U.S. rights under the Monroe Doctrine (1823) to prevent this circumstance from happening.

The situation in Cuba was tense because, having just finished its revolution, it was not exactly stable. Still, the communists in Cuba continued to ride a wave of popularity and Cuban armed forces were enthusiastic, if not well-trained. Fidel Castro was no friend of the United States; after all, the Kennedy administration had tried to overthrow him in the failed Bay of Pigs invasion (April 1961), and it was fairly obvious to all that he was a true communist. The United States decided to undertake action to prevent the further placement of nuclear missiles in Cuba, by military force if necessary.

What the Americans did not know was that the Soviets already had nuclear weapons in Cuba, which they planned to use to repel a possible invasion—this fact only became known in the West after the Cold War ended. Soviet doctrine allowed for the use of, and a willingness to use, tactical nuclear weapons in these circumstances. Of course, their use would have caused a general, almost undoubtedly nuclear, war. At the same time, the U.S. Army was preparing an invasion from Florida—moving tens of thousands of men and tons of matériel to the state—and was ready to attack if called upon. Both sides were ready for a confrontation.

Hawks on both sides pushed for war, even the possible use of nuclear weapons. Many people within the defense establishment believed that the best way to deal with the Soviet Union was to launch an all-out attack, including nuclear weapons, in a first strike. This assault would decide the Cold War all at once, in their opinion, and the victorious West could move on.

U.S. Air Force general Curtis E. LeMay, the architect of the most devastating air attacks in history—the fire bombing of Tokyo (9–10 March 1945)—and the nuclear attacks. in Japan (August 1945), had no qualms about nuclear war. He believed not only that it was possible to win a nuclear

Kennedy Tried to "Know His Enemy"

Robert F. Kennedy, the president's brother and his attorney general, describes Kennedy's efforts to understand Khrushchev's actions during the crisis.

The final lesson of the Cuban missile crisis is the importance of placing ourselves in the other country's shoes. During the crisis, President Kennedy spent more time trying to determine the effect of a particular course of action on Khrushchev or the Russians than on any other phase of what he was doing. What guided all his deliberations was an effort not to disgrace Khrushchev, not to humiliate the Soviet Union, not to have them feel they would have to escalate their response because their national security or national interests so committed them.

This was why he was so reluctant to stop and search a Russian ship; this was why he was so opposed to attacking the missile sites. The Russians, he felt, would have to react militarily to such actions on our part.

Thus the initial decision to impose a quarantine rather than to attack; our decision to permit the *Bucharest* to pass; our decision to board a non-Russian vessel first; all these and many more were taken with a view to putting pressure on the Soviet Union but not causing a public humiliation.

Miscalculation and misunderstanding and escalation on one side bring a counterresponse. No action is taken against a powerful adversary in a vacuum. A government or people will fail to understand this only at their great peril.

exchange, but that the resulting millions of friendly casualties from such a confrontation would be acceptable. On the Soviet side, there also were many hawks who wanted war, especially since they believed that the United States would invade Cuba. While Nikita S. Khrushchev did not

---

For that is how wars begin—wars that no one wants, no one intends, and no one wins.

Each decision that President Kennedy made kept this in mind. Always he asked himself: Can we be sure that Khrushchev understands what we feel to be our vital national interest? Has the Soviet Union had sufficient time to react soberly to a particular step we have taken? All action was judged against that standard—stopping a particular ship, sending low-flying planes, making a public statement.

President Kennedy understood that the Soviet Union did not want war, and they understood that we wished to avoid armed conflict. Thus, if hostilities were to come, it would be either because our national interests collided— which, because of their limited interests and our purposely limited objectives, seemed unlikely—or because of our failure or their failure to understand the other's objectives.

President Kennedy dedicated himself to making it clear to Khrushchev by word and deed—for both are important—that the U.S. had limited objectives and that we had no interest in accomplishing those objectives by adversely affecting the national security of the Soviet Union or by humiliating her.

Later, he was to say in his speech at American University in June of 1963: "Above all, while defending our own vital interests, nuclear powers must avert those confrontations which bring an adversary to the choice of either a humiliating defeat or a nuclear war."

Robert F. Kennedy, *Thirteen Days: A Memoir of the Cuban Missile Crisis.* New York: W.W. Norton, 1969, pp. 124–26.

agree, he was willing to fight if necessary. Clearly both sides were "eyeball to eyeball."

The situation escalated, however, when the Cubans shot down a U-2 reconnaissance aircraft on a spy mission in their airspace. Cuba was perfectly within its rights to do this as the overflight was a violation of its national sovereignty. The fact that the United States did not know that Cuban air defenses were capable of this action and the pilot was killed only added ammunition to the hawks in Washington.

There was only one method short of war, however, to prevent the placement of nuclear missiles in Cuba—a blockade, which is in fact an of of war. On the other hand, a "quarantine" (a blockade by another name) is not. By "quarantining" Cuba the United States could achieve its goal, using an extreme measure without the negative consequences attached to it. Still, the strategy was dangerous, for both sides clearly lad no real idea of the motives or resolve of heir opponents. The Kennedy administration announced that U.S. naval forces would stop, board, and search ships approaching Cuba in international waters and turn back those carrying offensive weapons. While this was a more "peaceful" solution, Kennedy made it clear that he would attack Cuba if the missiles already on the island were not removed.

Nevertheless, during the crisis the leadership in the United States and the Soviet Union realized that they were on the brink of a nuclear exchange and that, if they wanted to avoid it, they would have to negotiate. The problem was that they were so used to being enemies, after the end of World War II, that they did not really know how to talk to each other, especially since this situation had already proved how incorrect their concepts of each other were. Despite these difficulties, however, they negotiated.

The Soviet position, that they had a right to place missiles in Cuba, was not unreasonable as the United States had medium-range nuclear missiles in Europe pointed directly at the Union of Soviet Socialist Republics (U.S.S.R.). The reality was that the Soviets were simply doing what the Americans had already done and they misjudged U.S. intelligence capabilities, never expecting to get caught. Further, Khrushchev was honestly surprised by the U.S. reaction, for he had miscalculated U.S. resolve in this matter. Again, this blunder only demonstrates how little the two sides understood the motives and goals of the other.

Both sides worked together, for the first time since World War II, for a common goal and a common good, and reached equitable terms. The Soviets agreed to publicly pull out their nuclear weapons from Cuba, while the United States said it would secretly remove its medium-range missiles from Turkey. This agreement was a victory for both sides. The United States was able to save face with the secrecy clause, while the U.S.S.R. got the Americans to remove their weapons from the Soviet border.

In all, the crisis was successful in that both sides walked away from it with concessions at the cost of few lives. There was no world war, and the crisis set the stage for future relations. The United States and the U.S.S.R. came to the realization that having these weapons on the border of their enemy was a dangerous and destabilizing strategy. They also discovered that they needed greater communication with each other to prevent these misunderstandings and avoid a nuclear conflict. Finally, they recognized that perhaps they should consider working together to reduce their vast nuclear stockpiles.

Yet the United States and Soviet Union did not become friends after this incident. Both sides intensified their efforts to nullify the actions of the other, but with less directly confrontational means. The Soviets gave greater support to countries fighting U.S. interests, while the Americans reciprocated, giving rise to fighting each other by proxy.

The Soviets also made some crucial military decisions as a result of this confrontation. Most notably, they recognized that the U.S. quarantine was effective because the Soviet navy was unable to compete with its U.S. counterpart. This realization led to an intense period of naval construction in the Soviet Union to create a truly blue-water navy that could deal with this newly discerned threat. The Cold War was not over after the Cuban Missile Crisis, but the crisis was the last time that both sides stood on their highest nuclear alert status.

Kennedy's Idealism Led to U.S. Involvement in Vietnam

Richard J. Walton

In an effort to contain the spread of communism and to diminish the influence of the Soviet Union in Asia, Kennedy expanded U.S. military support for South Vietnam. At first, this included small numbers of military advisers and increased equipment and supplies. However, Kennedy's policy would culminate in the Vietnam War. Richard J. Walton contends that Kennedy appreciated the risks of U.S. military intervention in Vietnam, but that the president sincerely believed that American ideals of democracy and liberty could overcome Vietnamese nationalism. Kennedy also thought that the American presence could ameliorate the corruption of the regime in Saigon. Walton was a reporter and author who taught at the New School for Social Research in New York and Western Connecticut State College. He served as the Voice of America correspondent for the United Nations from 1962 to 1967.

ALTHOUGH THE CUBAN MISSILE CRISIS WAS THE MOST dangerous moment of the Kennedy administration, it is now but a dramatic episode in the history of the nation and in the personal histories of those who lived through those anxious thirteen days. Vietnam is Kennedy's

Richard J. Walton, "Vietnam," *Cold War and Counterrevolution: The Foreign Policy of John F. Kennedy.* New York: Viking Press, 1972. Copyright © 1972 by Richard J. Walton. All rights reserved. Reproduced by permission of Viking Penguin, a division of Penguin Group Inc.

most lasting legacy, and the sad irony is that Kennedy was one of the first American political figures to perceive in the early 1950s the difficulty of United States intervention. As early as 1951 young Congressman John Kennedy journeyed to Asia and on his return, warned that "in Indochina we have allied ourselves with a colonial regime that had no real support from the people." And in April 1954, when President Eisenhower was moving toward his decision not to try a last-ditch rescue of the French at Dienbienphu, Senator Kennedy took the floor to warn of the dangers of intervention. . . .

Yet even while Kennedy recognized the difficulties, the anti-communist triumphed over the realist, or perhaps it would be more accurate to say that the anti-communist confused the realist!

> To check the southern drive of communism makes sense but not only through reliance on the force of arms. The task is rather to build strong native non-communist sentiment within these areas and rely on that as a spearhead of defense rather than upon the legions of General de Tassigny. To do this apart from and in defiance of innately nationalistic aims spells fore-doomed failure.

This was Kennedy's crucial misconception. He recognized the irresistible force of nationalism, yet he believed it could be exploited from outside to defeat communism. He believed that the United States could manipulate the strong emotions of a downtrodden people so as to enlist them in America's crusade, not theirs. Much misery has resulted from the inability of John Kennedy, and other American leaders before him and since, to recognize that communism is not a monolithic, indivisible force. Communism and nationalism can be synonymous, as they have been with Ho Chi Minh or Tito or, later, Castro or, most important, Mao Tse-tung, but whatever their rhetoric, whatever their devotion to the principles of Marxism-Leninism, these communist leaders always put their countries first. . . .

Between 1951, when he was a young congressman, and 1961, when he was President, still young but presumably sophisticated and pragmatic, Kennedy did not learn that essential lesson. This is not so surprising when one considers that it was learned by very few people indeed. Americans seemed unable to recognize that a people, in the exercise of their national fervor, might want a communist to lead them. With that profound, matter-of-fact arrogance that America knows best, Eisenhower and Dulles chose Ngo Dinh Diem to lead South Vietnam, and Kennedy later decided, until he changed his mind toward the end, to keep him in power. It was Americans, not Vietnamese, who chose Diem. And it was Americans, not Vietnamese, who were surprised when Diem acted like an autocratic despot. . . .

Developing a Policy

When Kennedy was a candidate for presidential office, Vietnam was not a preoccupation with him. In the index to the collection of his campaign speeches from August 1 to Election Day, Vietnam is listed only twice and all Indochina only nine times. It was Cuba that was his major concern during his first months in office. But soon he had to consider the deteriorating situation in Vietnam. There were two prescriptions offered by his advisers: one predominantly military, the other predominantly political. These led to internal conflict, "and the struggle within the administration became increasingly bitter," McGeorge Bundy calling Vietnam "the most divisive issue in the Kennedy administration." But the dispute was one of tactics; one searches in vain throughout the wide literature available to find any substantial debate as to whether the United States had any business being in Vietnam in the first place. . . .

In those first months the Kennedy administration groped for a strategic concept. One, which at least had the virtue of consistency, was Walt W. Rostow's suggestion that "the ultimate source of aggression" should be attacked. Members of the Kennedy and Johnson administrations consistently spoke of "aggression from the North" and resolutely refused to face the elementary fact that the war in Vietnam was a civil war. . . .

Another "strategic concept" for Vietnam also featured police and military measures. "But the approach was essentially political. What was needed to meet the guerrilla threat successfully, we felt, were reformers to organize mass parties and social and political programs that could become the basis for modernization." This plan overlooked the fact that this ground had already been staked out by Ho Chi Minh and the communists. An arrogant, dictatorial mandarin such as Ngo Dinh Diem, a militant Catholic in a Buddhist land, was hardly likely to be a passionate reformer. And it should be noted that Kennedy's "liberal" administration wanted reforms not primarily for their benefits to the Vietnamese people but because they would strengthen the Diem regime's capacity to fight the war.

American Involvement

Shortly after he took office, Kennedy was shocked by a report on Vietnam prepared not long before by General Edward Lansdale, a shadowy but legendary officer with the CIA . . . Lansdale reported that despite seven years of United States economic, logistic, and political assistance, the Viet Cong was rapidly gaining strength and controlling increasing areas of the countryside. Kennedy decided that something had to be done. He quickly relieved Ambassador Elbridge Dubrow, who had carried so many complaints to Diem from the Eisenhower administration that he was no longer welcome at the Presidential Palace, and replaced him with Frederick Nolting, a nice comfortable foreign-service officer whose assignment was to win Diem's confidence and persuade him to undertake the reforms that would justify continued American support. He was to succeed fully in the first assignment and to fail completely in the second.

Meanwhile, Kennedy agreed to increase the number of American military advisers in Vietnam—about 600 when he took office—and to step up economic and military aid programs. His own task force recommended combat troops, but he settled on the increase of advisers. These, however, now served on the battalion as well as the regimental level and could advise on combat, on both the conventional and unconventional levels, as well as on training. On April 29, 1961, just days after the Bay of Pigs fiasco and while the crisis in Laos was at a crucial stage, he approved the recommendation for a 100-man increase in American advisers and some additional logistical support. . . . This was the first step in an escalation that was to continue throughout the Kennedy years. And as the papers pointed out, publicity would have entailed "the first formal breach of the Geneva agreements," so the move was kept quiet. This, too, established a pattern followed by Kennedy and his successors. The public was either not informed or actually deceived.

In May, Kennedy sent Vice President Lyndon Johnson to Saigon, partly to get an independent report, partly to assure Diem of his support, and partly to put pressure on Diem to carry out the reforms that always died somewhere between the agreement and the execution. Even while Johnson was still on his trip, in fact only a couple of days after he left, Kennedy decided to accept a further recommendation that 400 Special Forces troops (later known better as Green Berets) be sent to Vietnam to carry on covert warfare. As recorded in National Security Action Memorandum 52, Kennedy also instructed that the following steps be carried out:

1. "Dispatch . . . agents to North Vietnam" for intelligence gathering.

2. "Infiltrate teams under light civilian cover to southeast Laos to locate and attack Vietnamese communist bases and lines of communications."

3. "In North Vietnam, using the foundation established by intelligence operations, form networks of resistance,

---

Kennedy Was Searching for a "Nonmilitary" Approach to Vietnam

According to the eminent historian and former Kennedy aide Arthur M. Schlesinger Jr., by 1963, Kennedy had begun to reevaluate American military assistance to South Vietnam.

Kennedy had no intention of dispatching American ground forces to save South Vietnam. Nor did he accept the Truman-Eisenhower-Pentagon view that a President had inherent authority to send an expeditionary force into battle. If combat troops "in the generally understood sense of the word"— units, not advisers—were required in Vietnam, he told a press conference in March 1962, that would be "a basic change . . . which calls for a constitutional decision, [and] of course I would go to the Congress." As for counterinsurgency, if he believed it had any chance of licking the Viet Cong, he would surely have pushed it harder than he did. . . .

As against both win-the-war factions, Kennedy, I believe, was vaguely searching for a nonmilitary solution— vaguely because Vietnam was still a side show. In April 1962 [Kennedy confidant John Kenneth] Galbraith proposed that the United States offer "phased withdrawal" (there were then about 2000 troops in Vietnam) as an element in a larger deal with the Soviet Union, which in return might get Hanoi to call off the Viet Cong. Kennedy asked Defense for comment. After sneers at the idea of a "political solution," the chairman of the JCS [Joint Chiefs of Staff], General Lyman Lemnitzer, denounced Galbraith for wishing the United States "to seek disengagement from what is now a covert bases and teams for sabotage and light harassment."

4. "Conduct overflights for dropping of leaflets to harass the communists and to maintain morale of North Vietnamese population, and increase gray [unidentified-source] broadcasts to North Vietnam for the same purposes."

---

well-known commitment to take a forthright stand against Communism in Southeast Asia."

For the Chiefs the commitment may have been "well-known." But they had thus far failed in their efforts to force it on the President. A few days later a George Ball [Kennedy's Undersecretary of State] speech stimulated the militant Marguerite Higgins to lead her *Herald Tribune* story: "American retreat or withdrawal from South Viet-Nam is unthinkable, according to Mr. Ball. The American commitment, moreover, is now irrevocable." Ball, making a case, as lawyers do for clients—privately he opposed American involvement—portrayed the possible downfall of South Vietnam as "a loss of tragic significance to the security of free world interests in the whole of Asia and the South Pacific." Kennedy, disturbed, asked [National Security Advisor McGeorge] Bundy how Ball's disquisition had slipped by. The speech, Bundy informed the President, had "a tone and content that we would not have cleared, simply from the point of view of maintaining a chance of political settlement."

In July 1962, despite the Joint Chiefs' excommunication of Galbraith, Kennedy instructed [Secretary of Defense Robert] McNamara to start planning for the phased withdrawal of American military personnel from Vietnam. The assumption was that South Vietnamese troops would take up the slack as their capabilities improved under American training. The target date for complete disengagement was the end of 1965.

Arthur M. Schlesinger Jr., *Robert Kennedy and His Times*. Boston: Houghton Mifflin, 1978, pp. 708–709.

5. Train "the South Vietnamese Army to conduct ranger raids and similar military actions in North Vietnam as might prove necessary or appropriate."

Most important, Kennedy instructed Johnson to "encourage" Diem to request American ground troops. Diem's initial response to the secret urging was to decline. He said that he did not want United States troops except in the case of direct aggression by North Vietnam, pointing out that such troops would violate the 1954 Geneva accords. Later, Diem wrote to Kennedy that he wanted increased material support, that the dispatch of United States troops would lend support to the communist charge that he was a front for American imperialists. However, with the military situation continuing to deteriorate, Diem in October did ask for United States troops.

Exercising his Texan's talent for hyperbole, Johnson proclaimed Diem as "the Winston Churchill of Southeast Asia." On his return to Washington, Johnson told the President that time was running out and a basic decision had to be made. "We must decide whether to help these countries to the best of our ability or throw in the towel in the area and pull back our defenses to San Francisco and a 'Fortress America' concept. More important, we would say to the world in this case that we don't live up to our treaties and don't stand by our friends. This is not my concept. I recommend that we move forward promptly with a major effort to help these countries defend themselves."

But that May, Kennedy got advice based on much longer experience in Vietnam, advice that, had it been taken, would have prevented an indelible stain on Kennedy's record. Infinitely more important, it probably would have spared the people of Indochina incalculable death, destruction, and pain and spared America not only the lives of 50,000 men but the turmoil and divisiveness caused by the Vietnam war. On May 31, 1961, Kennedy, en route to his Vienna talks with Khrushchev, stopped in Paris for a couple of days to see

Charles de Gaulle. The old French President urged his young American counterpart to learn from France's misfortune and not become entangled in Vietnam. . . .

In his memoirs, De Gaulle added these sad, prophetic words: "Kennedy is listening to me, but events will show that I did not convince him." Khrushchev, a couple of days later, said these same things, but Kennedy, to his terrible loss and ours, paid heed to neither adversary nor ally.

Counterinsurgency

While it was the Johnson trip to Saigon that got the headlines, a more important visit was made by Professor Eugene Staley of the Stanford Research Institute. Working closely with Ngo Dinh Nhu, Diem's brother, closest adviser, and head of the secret-police apparatus, Staley developed the idea of "strategic hamlets." It was a welcome idea in Washington, where Kennedy's enthusiasm for "counterinsurgency" was spreading. The President was an avid reader of Mao Tse-tung and Ernesto "Che" Guevara, and the strategic hamlets seemed to be the way to deprive the Viet Cong guerrillas of the people. Mao, had written that "guerrillas must move among the people as fish swim in the sea." According to the Nhu-Staley plan, the peasants would work in the fields by day, and by night, when the Viet Cong normally exerted its control, the peasants would move into the safety of the strategic hamlets. This would deprive, so it was thought, the Viet Cong of essential food, supplies, and shelter. It was an ingenious plan. . . .

Although the strategic-hamlet program had some success at first, it eventually suffered the fate of all the other ingenious schemes devised in Washington and Saigon that promised an early and successful end to the war. In every case—the concentrated use of helicopters, the bombing of the North, the invasions of Cambodia and Laos—the Viet Cong has learned how to cope. Either that or the plans turned out to have inherent faults, in theory or execution, so that in the long run none of these "miracles" worked.

The strategic hamlets were part of a wider Kennedy program of counterinsurgency. Indeed, that term became a watchword in Washington during the Kennedy years. The President set up an interdepartmental counterinsurgency committee under one of his favorite advisers, General Maxwell Taylor, with his brother, the Attorney General, as his personal representative on the committee.... The Pentagon, reluctantly, the CIA, State, and the United States Information Agency were all involved. Special counterinsurgency schools were set up in Washington, and it was a mark of favor to be sent to one; bureaucrats scrambled frantically for such preferment.

Kennedy did not count on the Special Forces to win guerrilla wars abroad.... Such an effort was doomed from the beginning. An effective guerrilla movement can be successfully countered only by the adoption of programs that remove the grievances that caused the guerrillas to take the field in the first place. Kennedy and his top advisers were right in recognizing that widespread reform was necessary in South Vietnam but naïve in expecting that Diem, who had perpetuated the intolerable conditions, would carry out such reforms. Diem was only acting true to his nature in responding with repression to the people's—and the Americans'—demands for reform....

The Situation Deteriorates

Throughout 1961 the situation in Vietnam continued to deteriorate. Theodore H. White, the journalist close to many in the Kennedy administration, wrote to Washington in August: "... The guerrillas now control almost all the southern delta—so much so that I could find no American who would drive me outside Saigon in his car even by day without military convoy." He reported "political breakdown of formidable proportions" and then raised the essential point: "... what perplexes hell out of me is that the

Commies, on their side, seem to be able to find people willing to die for their cause." If nothing else could persuade Kennedy to stay out of Vietnam, this should have. If there is any absolute test of the strength of a cause, it is whether or not men willingly sacrifice their lives for it. Men were willing to die for the cause personified by Ho Chi Minh; they were not willing to die for that personified by Ngo Dinh Diem. It was as simple as that. If Diem could not recruit effective support from among his own people, he did not deserve support from outside, nor would outside support, at any reasonable level, do any good.

In October Kennedy sent Maxwell Taylor and Walt Rostow to Saigon. They came back with a report that the situation was serious but not hopeless. They recommended increased economic assistance, a step-up in military advisers, the use of Americans for airlift and air reconnaissance operations, even the dispatch of as many as 10,000 combat troops. They noted Diem's shortcomings but specifically rejected the idea of his being replaced. John Kenneth Galbraith was also asked to stop in Saigon on his way back from Washington to his post as Ambassador to India. He wrote that there was not "the slightest practical chance" that the reforms being urged on Diem would be carried out and that any long-term success would depend on Diem's being replaced.

Nonetheless, Kennedy had faith in Taylor and Rostow—and in McNamara, who concurred with their views. So he followed their recommendations, except for sending the combat troops. His reason for not sending the combat troops was sadly prophetic.

> . . . They want a force of American troops. They say it's necessary to restore confidence and maintain morale. But it will be just like Berlin. The troops will march in; the bands will play; the crowds will cheer; and in four days everyone will have forgotten. Then we will be told

we have to send in more troops. It's like taking a drink.
The effect wears off, and you have to take another.

That autumn of 1961 is, for several reasons, crucial to any study of the Kennedy administration and the Vietnam war. On October 5 a special national intelligence estimate reported "that 80–90 per cent of the estimated 17,000 VC had been locally recruited, and that there was little evidence that the VC relied on external supplies." Even if one were to accept the Kennedy administration's indefensible contention that the war was an international one between two different nations, the administration's own figures show that there was little help from the North, certainly nothing to compare in even the remotest degree with American aid to the South. Blaming Hanoi for the collapsing situation in South Vietnam was simply a smokescreen to hide the fact that Diem was being defeated by foes within his own half of the country, with little outside help. In order to justify further aid to Diem, it was necessary for the Kennedy administration to provoke the old American conditioned reflex to the menace of communism. If the American people came to realize that Diem's large, well-equipped army (paid for, supplied, and trained by the United States) was being defeated by a few thousand rebels, it might come to feel that Diem did not deserve help. But if Diem was the victim of "communist aggression"—well, that was different.

Yet even though Kennedy was willing to reawaken old fears, as he had done in his campaign and did with Laos and Cuba after taking office, he did not want the people to know precisely what he was doing. He certainly did not want them to realize that the United States was slipping deeper and deeper into the Indochinese quagmire. Thus, when the press began to ask whether Maxwell Taylor's trip to Saigon meant that Kennedy was considering sending combat troops to Vietnam, the administration deliberately—and successfully—set out to deceive the press and the public. . . .

Consequence of Failure

If one accepts the view that the United States was right to intervene in a civil war, such intervention could be justified only if there were a reasonable chance of success. Success depended, as Kennedy and all his top advisers recognized, on substantial reforms. Yet Kennedy in December 1961 backed down on his demand for reforms; he was not prepared to tell a stubborn Diem: Reform or else. And having backed down then, Kennedy was not able later to convince Diem, at an even more critical moment, that he meant it when he insisted on essential reforms. Because of the supremacy of the Pentagon over the State Department, Kennedy already tended to see Vietnam as more of a military than a political problem. Since Diem was fairly cooperative on military matters and stubborn on political, the Kennedy administration concentrated on the symptom (the Vietcong rebellion) and not on the cause—Diem's repressive, corrupt rule. This was perhaps inevitable, given Kennedy's preoccupation with communism, but he was hardly alone. Truman and Eisenhower before him and Johnson and Nixon after him were the same. Their first concern was not the welfare of whatever people were involved, but in smashing communism or later, when that proved impossible, in saving face. The irony, of course, is that they would have been more effective had they been more concerned with the people and less with ideology. . . .

In his 1963 State of the Union message, Kennedy said on January 14 that the "spearpoint of aggression has been blunted in Vietnam." But the President preferred not to talk about Vietnam any more than he had to. He hardly wanted to tell the American people that the Diem regime almost entirely rejected the reforms that could have justified it as a government, that the United States was supporting a corrupt, repressive, incompetent regime.

CHAPTER

2

HUMAN RIGHTS
AND PEACE

Kennedy Used Humanitarian Aid as a Means to Counter Communism

Seyom Brown

Kennedy understood that the United States could not simply rely on military assistance to ensure that pro-U.S. governments resisted communism or alliance with the Soviet Union. Therefore, he consistently sought to develop programs, such as the Peace Corps, that would provide nonmilitary assistance to developing nations. By the time of his assassination, Kennedy had initiated a number of aid programs, including the Alliance for Progress, to improve the economies of underdeveloped states. Seyom Brown contends that the alliance had mixed results, partially because of misunderstandings about Latin America and partially because of factors beyond the control of the United States, mainly population growth and regime corruption. Brown is the Lawrence A. Wien Professor of International Cooperation at Brandeis University. He has published a number of works on U.S. foreign policy and international relations.

———————————————— ■ ————————————————

A NALYSTS WITH AN ORIENTATION TOWARD MILITARY AF-fairs are prone to pay most attention to the so-called Kennedy-McNamara "revolution" in military policy, as if it

Seyom Brown, *The Faces of Power: United States Foreign Policy from Truman to Clinton.* New York: Columbia University Press, 1994. Copyright © 1994 by Columbia University Press. All rights reserved. Reproduced by permission.

were the centerpiece of the Kennedy administration's foreign policy. But this is to confuse immediacy with high value. At the center of the Kennedy foreign policy was the premise that the competition between the Soviet Union and the United States was shifting to a new arena competition for influence over the direction of development in the poorer half of the globe; and it was in respect to this competition that the United States was in greatest danger of falling behind.

In his pre–White House years, Kennedy turned much of his fire on the Eisenhower-Dulles approach to the Third World. The Middle East, particularly, had been the scene or "grave errors":

> We overestimated our own strength and underestimated the force of nationalism. . . . We gave our support to regimes instead of to people—and too often we tied our future to the fortunes of unpopular and ultimately overthrown governments and rulers.

> We believed that those governments which were friendly to us and hostile to the Communists were therefore good governments—and we believed that we could make unpopular policies acceptable through our own propaganda programs. . . .

A New Approach to Aid

For "terms that go beyond the vocabulary of the Cold War" Kennedy went to his economist friends. They were putting together a doctrine on the relationship between the structure of societies, the availability of external capital, and the modernization process. . . . There were the expected intellectual disagreements among learned men of an inexact science; but there was a notable convergence on a set of propositions with important implications for concrete policy.

• The objective of assistance to the underdeveloped nations should be to help them achieve a condition in which economic growth is a normal and self-sustaining process within a democratic political system.

• The attainment of a condition of self-sustaining growth for most of the underdeveloped nations will require fundamental modifications of the economic *and* noneconomic structures of their societies.

• Putting off the fundamental societal modifications until popular demands for change have risen to a high pitch would likely lead to violent upheavals followed by totalitarian rule.

• The required structural modifications can be accomplished peacefully if they are begun early, and are translated into carefully coordinated attacks on the particular roadblocks to modernization found in each nation.

Frequently occurring roadblocks are: (1) a lack of sufficient agricultural productivity beyond the subsistence level (sufficient productivity is an important source of investment capital formation); (2) a lack of sufficient investment in social overhead projects (transportation and communication networks especially); (3) the lack of indigenous specialists able to administer these development tasks and to train the rural population in modes of greater productivity; (4) the lack of literacy, which does not allow for the absorption of new values and techniques (including population control) by the population; and (5) the lack of sufficient commitment on the part of elites to greater economic egalitarianism and political democracy. . . .

• Military or ideological alignment with the United States should not be a prominent criterion for the flow of assistance.

Many of the scholars involved in generating these propositions were now brought into the government—on the White House staff, the State Department, and as ambassadors to important underdeveloped countries. . . . From their point of view, and from Kennedy's, they had practically a carte blanche opportunity to reorganize the entire foreign assistance program, its personnel as well as its operational guidelines. A large new foreign aid program for Latin America was to be funded where the new premises would have a proving ground, unencumbered by existing programmatic commitments. . . .

Beyond the Cold War?

President Kennedy's appreciation of the highly insecure political base of the leaders of the developing nations led him to expunge cold war rhetoric, as much as possible, from the public rationale for foreign assistance. He responded positively to the suggestions to tone down the anti-Communist appeals appearing in the first draft of his March 1961 foreign aid message. From the outset, however, he was the focal point of the tension between two "constituencies" of the foreign assistance program: the overseas recipients of assistance (whose Washington champions were the development economists in Kennedy's advisory entourage); and, opposing them, the neo-isolationist elements in the American electorate, in portions of the business community, and in segments of organized labor whose congressional brokers have traditionally coalesced to prune administration foreign assistance requests not carrying a simple "essential for national security" rationale. . . .

As revealed by Arthur Schlesinger, Jr. (who was heavily involved as a consultant to Kennedy on Latin American affairs), the cold war was a pervasive part of the discussions in the White House on the Latin American aid program. Kennedy's interregnum task force on Latin America emphasized the Communist threat, describing it as "more dangerous than the Nazi-Fascist threat [to Latin America] of the Franklin Roosevelt period. . . ." The objective of the Communists, said the task force report, was "to convert the Latin American social revolution into a Marxist attack on the

United States itself." As this revolution was "inevitable and necessary," the way to counter the Communist threat was to "divorce" the Latin American social transformation "from connection with and prevent its capture by Communist power politics." The United States needed to put itself clearly on the side of the indigenous "democratic-progressive movements . . . pledged to representative government and economic reform (including agrarian reform) and resistance to entrance of undemocratic forces from outside the hemisphere."

Alianza

After the Kennedy inauguration the momentum for a new departure to Latin American policy accelerated. . . .

The "solution," as exhibited in the President's proposal of March 13, 1961, for "a vast new ten-year plan for the Americas," was a coupling of the structural approach to economic development that had been advanced by . . . economists with the revolutionary idealism of Thomas Jefferson and Simón Bolívar. Kennedy christened the *Alianza* the contemporary expression of the American revolution (North and South) for the rights of man:

> Our nations are the product of a common struggle—the revolt from colonial rule.
>
> . . .
>
> The revolutions which gave us birth ignited, in the words of Thomas Paine, "a spark never to be extinguished.". . . we must remember that . . . the revolution which began in 1776 and in Caracas in 1811 . . . is not yet finished. Our hemisphere's mission is not yet completed. *For our unfulfilled task is to demonstrate to the entire world that man's unsatisfied aspiration for economic progress and social justice can best be achieved by free men working within a framework of democratic institutions.*

The concrete steps "to complete the revolution of the Americas" were to be presented in detail at a ministerial meeting of the Inter-American Economic and Social Council. But the President's speech gave a preview of the criteria which

---

Congress Resisted the Expansion of Foreign Aid

According to Kennedy scholar Richard J. Walton, although greater foreign assistance was a priority for Kennedy, he consistently found that Congress sought to decrease aid in order to spend more on domestic programs.

President Kennedy wanted to spend more money on foreign aid, not only because he believed in it for its own sake but because he saw it as an essential counter to communism. But foreign aid during the Kennedy years was cut as never before. For fiscal 1963, for instance, he asked Congress for $4.9 billion. By the time Congress got through with his request—despite an intensive campaign in its behalf—it was slashed to $3.2 billion, the largest cut in the history of foreign aid. It is hard to say why. Perhaps Congress, which had always had to be bludgeoned into large foreign-aid appropriations, had finally tired of spending huge sums that seemed to profit the United States little. Perhaps it had wearied of the argument, pushed again by Kennedy, that foreign aid was a bulwark against communism. Certainly it had never been much impressed by the argument that it was the obligation of the United States to help the poorer nations. Nor was it even persuaded by the argument that it was in the national interest not to let the gap between the rich and poor nations grow. Probably a sense of disillusion over Vietnam contributed. Whatever the reason, this was a bitter defeat for Kennedy.

Richard J. Walton, *Cold War and Counterrevolution: The Foreign Policy of John F. Kennedy.* New York: Viking Press, 1972, pp. 216–17.

his administration would insist be applied in evaluating a potential recipient's commitments to the ideals of the unfinished hemispheric revolution. Political freedom, said the President, had to accompany material progress, but political freedom must be accomplished by social change:

> For unless necessary social reforms, including land and tax reform, are freely made, unless we broaden the opportunity, of all our people, unless the great mass of Americans share in increasing prosperity then our alliance, our revolution, our dream, and our freedom will fail.

This approach was a product of the analysis of the New Frontiersmen that the weakest chink in the armor of the non-Communist world was the phenomenon of the entrenched oligarchy holding on to privilege in the face of rising demands for social justice. Identifying the United States with the current of social revolution would give it a legitimacy in these countries that would draw responsible professional and middle-class elements into the reform movements, and thereby channel pressures into practical demands and nonviolent modes of agitation. Furthermore, by providing an agenda of practical reforms and insisting that governments in these countries make discernible progress in this direction in order to qualify for development loans, the United States would be providing significant pressure from above to complement and reinforce the popular pressures it was encouraging from below. Progressive regimes would be strengthened against conservative elements in their societies; and oligarchical regimes would be squeezed in an ever-tightening vise.

If the Latin American nations took the necessary internal measures, Secretary of the Treasury Douglas Dillon told his fellow delegates at Punta del Este in August, they could reasonably expect their own efforts to be matched by an inflow of capital during the next decade amounting to at least $20 billion. The problem, he said, did not lie in a shortage of external capital, but "in organizing effective development programs so that both domestic and foreign capital can be put to work rapidly, wisely, and well." There were underlying principles to be adhered to: the loan recipients would have to dedicate larger proportions of their domestic resources to national development projects; integrated national programs for economic and social development would have to be formulated, setting forth goals and priorities to insure that available resources were used in the most effective manner, and such national development programs would have to be in accord with the right of all segments of the population to share fully in the fruits of progress. . . .

Tempered Enthusiasm

The assembled delegates of the Latin American republics, except for Cuba's Che Guevara, responded with enthusiasm to the United States initiative.

But it turned out to be an *Alianza* mainly at the level of verbalized aspiration. According to [Kennedy confidant and special counsel] Ted Sorensen, the President, after a year or so of little progress, was disappointed:

> what disturbed him most was the attitude of that 2 percent of the citizenry of Latin America who owned more than 50 percent of the wealth and controlled most of the political-economic apparatus. Their voices were influential, if not dominant, among the local governments, the armies, the newspapers and other opinion-makers. They had friendly ties with U.S. press and business interests who reflected their views in Washington. They saw no reason to alter the ancient feudal patterns of land tenure and tax structure, the top heavy military budgets, the substandard wages and the concentrations of capital. They classified many of their opponents as "communists," considered the social and political reforms of the *Alianza* a threat to stability and clung tenaciously to the status quo.

Moreover, even when there was the will to reform, there appeared to be a conspiracy of history, natural phenomena, and elemental human forces against essential change. The desire to effect at least a 2.5 percent per capita rate of economic growth just did not conform to the facts. A 3 percent per annum increase in the gross national product was very impressive for a Latin American country, yet with population growth running at 2.5 to 3 percent, the per capita increase was usually all but wiped out even in the best of cases. The lack of Latin American economists with experience in integrated national economic planning was another factor making for sluggishness. By the end of 1962 only five countries were able to submit national development plans for review, and of these only those submitted by Mexico and Venezuela were competently done and within the spirit of the *Alianza*. The lack of sufficiently studied and engineered projects meant that the United States government was able to disburse only two thirds of the $1.5 billion it had already pledged for the first year and a half of the program. Nor was the picture brightened by the worldwide drop in basic commodity prices—the major source of national income for most of the Latin American countries.

The Outcome

Was it all worth the effort anyway? Kennedy continued to think so, but without the earlier euphoria. He admitted that the Alliance for Progress "has failed to some degree because the problems are almost insuperable." In some ways, he said, "the road seems longer than it was when the journey started. But I think we ought to keep at it."

"Perhaps our most impressive accomplishment," said the President on the first anniversary of the Alliance for Progress, "has been the dramatic shift in thinking and attitudes which has occurred in our hemisphere":

Already elections are being fought in terms of the Alliance for Progress. . . . Already people throughout the hemisphere—in schools and in trade unions, in chambers of commerce and in military establishments, in government and on the farms—have accepted the goals of the charter as their own personal and political commitments. For the first time in the history of inter-American relations our energies are concentrated on the central task of democratic development.

This dramatic change in thought is essential to the realization of our goals.

The problem was that the dramatic change in thought, if unaccompanied by meaningful changes in government programs in these countries, could create an even larger gap between popular demands and government responsiveness, with governments in turn attempting to stifle demand, and the discontented turning in their frustration to insurgency. . . .

The people receiving money from the export of basic commodities were very often the same elements least interested in the social reform that would have to accompany true economic development in their countries.

The more conservative Latins, and United States interests, unsympathetic to the national planning approach and the emphasis upon public investment in the original conception of the Alliance, pointed to the decline in the flow of private capital to Latin America since Punta del Este. The obvious implication was that all the talk of dramatic social change, including drastic land and tax reforms, had raised the specter of confiscation of private holdings without sufficient compensation, harassment of foreign-subscribed private enterprise, and political instability leading to unpredictable radical economic experiments. . . . The forces for stability, recovering from the first shock of seeing the White House seriously identifying itself with the forces for change, had begun to regroup.

The Long Struggle

The President's response to the conservative counterattack was to show as much favor as possible to [progressive leaders in Latin America] and to point his finger at those Latin American forces which, in his view, constituted an alliance against progress:

> No amount of external resources, no stabilization of commodity prices, no new Inter-American institutions, can bring progress to nations which do not have political stability and determined leadership. No series of hemispheric agreements or elaborate machinery can help those who lack internal discipline, who are unwilling to make sacrifices and renounce privileges. No one who sends his money abroad, who is unwilling to invest in the future of his country, can blame others for the deluge which threatens to overcome and overwhelm him.

But the elements of lethargy, obstruction, and despair were not going to prevail this time, affirmed the President four days before his death. These forces should know that he was fully committed, and prepared for a long struggle. "Nothing is true except a man or men adhere to it—to live for it, to spend themselves on it, to die for it," he declaimed, quoting from a poem by Robert Frost.

The Alliance for Progress Failed to Help Latin America

Bruce Miroff

In 1961 Kennedy created the Alliance for Progress, a program designed to improve social and economic conditions and prevent violent revolution in Latin America. By 1963 it was clear that the program had failed to meet its goals. In the following selection, Bruce Miroff argues that although Kennedy's intentions to create a "democratic revolution" were genuine, the fundamental premises of the alliance were faulty. In the end, the alliance benefited only the interests of U.S. businesses and local elites. Miroff is a political historian and the author of *Icons of Democracy: American Leaders as Heroes, Aristocrats, Dissenters, and Democrats.*

J OHN F. KENNEDY'S RECORD IN THE THIRD WORLD WAS, ON the surface, a puzzling blend of the generous and the ignoble. Among Kennedy and his fellow New Frontiersmen, a sophisticated yet compassionate understanding of Third World problems seemed to exist. Marking that understanding were fresh departures in American foreign policy: the idealistic Peace Corps, a solicitous concern for the new nations of Africa, and, most notably, the Alliance for Progress campaign for economic development and so-

Bruce Miroff, *Pragmatic Illusions: The Presidential Politics of John F. Kennedy.* New York: David McKay, 1976. Copyright © 1976 by Bruce Miroff. Reproduced by permission. (Endnotes in the original have been omitted in this reprint.)

cial justice in Latin America. Yet, parallel to these undertakings was a history of repressive military intervention in the affairs of the Third World. Here, too, there were landmarks: the invasion of Cuba and the increasingly bitter struggle against the Viet Cong guerrillas in South Vietnam.

Doubtless there was genuine ambivalence in Kennedy's approach to the Third World, ambivalence fostered by a liberal's simultaneous desire for, and fear of, change. But ambivalence should not, in this case, be equated with inconsistency. For one consistent theme ran through almost all of Kennedy's ventures in the Third World—counterrevolution. Whatever other sympathies he professed, John Kennedy was a determined counterrevolutionary. His overriding aim was to banish the specter of radical revolution from the underdeveloped nations by channeling the forces of change into a "democratic revolution." The "democratic revolution" promised evolutionary change within a democratic framework, free from the disruption and violence of a radical social upheaval. It turned out to mean only the status quo in an elaborate new guise. . . .

The history of the Alliance for Progress can be recited relatively quickly; it takes only a few pages to describe its major events and achievements. What requires fuller consideration is the story of what didn't happen—the Alliance's glaring failure to fulfill its own goals or, indeed, to make even a dent in the stagnant economic and social order of the Latin American countries. That failure reveals much about the nature of present-day Latin America; it reveals far more about the political understanding of John Kennedy and his circle of advisers.

A New Hemispheric Revolution

The Alliance for Progress was hailed, when it was announced in March 1961, as the start of a new era in United States–Latin American relations. But reassessment of America's hemispheric policy had already begun in the Eisenhower Administration. After Vice-President [Richard] Nixon's ill-starred trip to South America in 1958, and the triumph of the Cuban revolution in 1959, Washington policy makers had observed with alarm the rising tide of discontent in an area long taken for granted. By 1960, they were agreed on the need to pour more energy and money into Latin America. At the Bogotá Conference the Eisenhower Administration thus pledged $500 million as an American "social progress fund" for Latin American development.

Despite Eisenhower's initiative, Kennedy as a presidential candidate considered the Republicans vulnerable on the subject of Latin America. He made it one of his key campaign issues, adopting the slogan "Alliance for Progress" (coined by [Deputy Secretary of State for Inter-American Affairs] Richard Goodwin) to describe his own prospective program. After his election, plans for this Alliance rapidly took form; by March 13, 1961, Kennedy was ready to unveil them to a White House assemblage of the Latin American diplomatic corps.

He painted his program in glowing terms. "I have called on all people of the hemisphere to join in a new Alliance for Progress—Alianza para Progreso—a vast cooperative effort, unparalleled in magnitude and nobility of purpose, to satisfy the basic needs of the American people for homes, work and land, health and schools. . . ." The new partnership of North and South would encompass both economic development and social restructuring—national planning and technical aid, agrarian reform and tax reform, public housing, education, and health care. And it would operate within the framework of democratic institutions, proving definitively the compatibility of representative government with material progress. Kennedy did not hesitate to call his Alliance a new hemispheric "revolution": "Let us once again transform the American continent into a vast crucible of revolutionary ideas and efforts. . . ."

The Alliance for Progress was born in hope, but also in

fear. Little was said about it at the time, yet it was apparent to everyone concerned that the Alliance was America's response to the Cuban revolution, its contrivance for heading off the eruption of Castro-style revolutions throughout the hemisphere. The rapid promulgation of this new Latin American policy betrayed the nightmare of Fidelismo at its base. "It was," Ronald Steel observed [in *Pax Americana*], "neither charity nor a guilty conscience but Fidel Castro who provided the inspiration for the Alliance for Progress.... The Alliance for Progress might never have seen the light of day, let alone grown into childhood, had Fidel not injected the fear of communism into official Washington."

Barely more than a month after the announcement of this program for forestalling copies of the Cuban revolution, Kennedy struck at the original. On April 17, a brigade of 1400 Cuban exiles under the direction of the CIA were set ashore at Cuba's Bay of Pigs. Their hope was to spark a general uprising against the Castro regime; if this did not occur in a few days the invaders could melt away into the mountains and commence guerrilla warfare. The CIA was highly optimistic about the scheme; Kennedy, while expressing some doubts, went along in the faith that the Cuban populace would rise up against what he himself had characterized as a government "seized by aliens." But in a matter of days the Cuban militia crushed the invasion force and took most of its members prisoner....

In the immediate aftermath of the Bay of Pigs ... Kennedy was too irate to hide the threat [of force which accompanied the Alliance].

Let the record show that our restraint is not inexhaustible. Should it ever appear that the inter-American doctrine of non-interference merely conceals or excuses a policy of nonaction—if the nations of this Hemisphere should fail to meet their commitments against outside Communist penetration—then I want it clearly understood that this Government will not hesitate in meeting its primary obligations which are to the security of our Nation!

The Kennedy Administration was soon eager to forget its blundering Cuban invasion. But for Latin Americans the invasion was not so easily forgotten; it remained a powerful object lesson in the U.S. response to social revolution in the hemisphere.

Lofty Goals

While Kennedy's popularity in Latin America sagged temporarily after the Bay of Pigs, hopes for the Alliance for Progress remained high. The Alliance was formally organized at a conference of the Inter-American Economic and Social Council held in Punta del Este, Uruguay, in August 1961. In his written message to this conference Kennedy returned to the generous purposes of his March speech. Profound changes in the social and economic structure of Latin America were again foretold: "For there is no place in democratic life for institutions which benefit the few while denying the needs of the many, even though the elimination of such institutions may require far-reaching and difficult changes such as land reform and tax reform and a vastly increased emphasis on education and health and housing." And a vast infusion of American care, as well as American money, was pledged: "Only an effort of towering dimensions—an effort similar to that which was needed to rebuild the economies of Western Europe—can ensure fulfillment of our Alliance for Progress."

Although some of the Latin American delegates to the conference were skeptical in private, publicly all (except Cuba's Che Guevara) endorsed the plans of Kennedy and his chief representative, Treasury Secretary Douglas Dillon. When the conference ended on August 17, those plans had been incorporated into an official Charter of Punta del Este. The ambitions of the Alliance can be seen in the social goals which the Charter set forth: comprehensive agrarian reform, tax reform, accelerated urban and rural housing development, accelerated programs of health and sanitation, elimination of illiteracy. The economic goals were equally ambitious: a national development plan for each country, fair wages, stable prices, Latin American economic integration, and a per capita growth rate of 2.5 percent a year. There was also a clear political goal: to protect and strengthen the institutions of representative democracy in the hemisphere. Toward all these ends the United States pledged $20 billion over the next ten years, slightly more than half in public assistance, the rest in private funds.

Dreary Failure

The history of the Alliance during the remainder of Kennedy's Presidency presents a dreary picture of inaction or failure. A year or two after Punta del Este the bright hopes of its founding had all but dissolved. Growth rates for the Latin American economies as a whole lagged far below the 2.5 percent figure. Land and tax reforms were, in most cases, hopelessly bottled up in conservative legislatures. As for the Alliance's commitment to democracy, the years 1962–63 witnessed repeated setbacks for democratic institutions in Latin America in the face of a resurgent militarism. In 1962 the governments of both Argentina and Peru were toppled by military coups; in 1963 four more governments—Guatemala, Ecuador, the Dominican Republic, and Honduras—fell under military control. These developments could not, of course, all be attributed to the Alliance. Still, it had rapidly become apparent that the Alliance could not live up to its name—and would not disturb Latin America's stagnation.

Confronted persistently with criticisms of the Alliance, Kennedy found it hard to disguise his gloom. All that he could do was to cite the difficulties that the Alliance faced—the complexity of Latin America's prob-

The Alliance for Progress
Faced a Variety of Hurdles

Historian Paul Y. Hammond describes some of the problems Kennedy encountered in both the creation and implementation of the Alliance for Progress.

Before a glittering audience of Latin American diplomats assembled in the White House in March 1961, Kennedy announced "a vast new 10-year plan for the Americas, a plan to transform the 1960's into a historic decade of democratic progress," repeatedly intoning the plan's Spanish name, *Alianza para Progreso*, in his flat Boston accent.

Latin America was changing rapidly. Its birth rate was the highest for any continent, its rate of urban growth phenomenal. Yet economic stagnation persisted. The Alliance, like the rest of the Kennedy Administration's economic-aid programs, gave primary attention to economic objectives, though from the beginning the political obstacles to economic development in Latin America proved particularly difficult to overcome. . . .

The Alliance needed to be sold in every participating country, including the United States. In the Latin American countries it could succeed only if it served as a rallying point for the supporters of change against the defenders of the status quo. Public figures in Latin America—to say nothing of the American Congress—who were potential supporters of the Alliance needed the encouragement and reassurance provided by publicity and political promotion, so that if they ventured to change things they could do so as part of a large and popular undertaking. For these reasons, it is not surprising that both the United States and the potential Latin American beneficiaries surrounded the Alliance with strong rhetorical flourishes—with a mystique.

Economic aid for the first year would be covered by the

$500 million left over from the Eisenhower Administration's Inter-American Fund for Social Progress. In his March 1962 foreign-aid message, Kennedy proposed $3 billion in development funds or the Alliance in the next four years, including $600 million for the fiscal year 1962–63. . . .

Since the United States and Latin America never fully agreed on Alliance objectives, however, bilateral aid remained a vital part of U.S. policy—and a persistent way to manipulate domestic politics in Latin America, as the experience with Brazil indicates. Brazil, the largest and most populous country in Latin America, had a federal form of government and relatively broad participation in its domestic politics. The defense of the status quo was maintained not merely by a narrow oligarchy but by a wide variety of political groups who benefited from the high rates of inflation under the status quo. In 1961 the United States discreetly supported the national assembly's successful effort to clip the powers of new Brazilian President Goulart when he seemed to be drifting to the left. Two years later, when Brazilian criticism of Goulart had declined and his constitutional powers had been restored. Washington provided $400 million in financial aid to help rescue the faltering financial structure of the Brazilian economy. Goulart, however, failed to cope with the mounting inflation—it climbed at the record pace of 100 percent in 1963—and the United States cancelled its assistance. The cancellation conformed to the Kennedy approach in economic assistance: setting and enforcing performance standards. But our action also amounted to using economic aid for political manipulation—the very thing the Kennedy economic assistance program was supposed to avoid. In practice it was hard to avoid sliding from one policy to the other.

Paul Y. Hammond, *The Cold War Years: American Foreign Policy Since 1945.* New York: Harcourt, Brace & World, 1969, pp. 189–91.

lems, its shortage of trained personnel to develop and administer reform programs, the opposition of vested interests to such programs—and to counsel patience. Sometimes even he found it difficult to follow that counsel. On the second anniversary of the Punta del Este conference, for example, he responded to a press conference query on Latin America with obvious frustration: "The problems are almost insuperable. . . ." Yet the grandiloquent rhetoric was never abandoned completely; four days before his death Kennedy declared: "The task we have set ourselves and the Alliance for Progress, the development of an entire continent, is a far greater task than any we have ever undertaken in our history."

At the time of Kennedy's death, supporters of the Alliance still could claim that its reforms would take hold in a few more years. By the end of the decade, those supporters had to admit that the critics had been right all along—by almost any standard imaginable the Alliance was a failure. None of the goals fixed at Punta del Este had been achieved. As Susanne Bodenheimer notes, figures compiled by the United Nations Economic Commission for Latin America actually show that "Latin America's problems of urban poverty, unemployment (particularly in rural areas), slow industrialization, inequalities of income and living standards, dependence upon foreign capital, foreign indebtedness, and slow expansion of foreign markets have become more critical during the [decade of the 1960's] . . . the annual average growth rate during the 1960's was lower than that of the previous decade and fell far short of targets established in 1961." Progress in land and tax reform was pathetically slow. Housing, sanitation, health care were no better for the great majority of Latin America's poor in 1970 than they had been in 1960. The fate of the Alliance could be summed up by its campaign against adult illiteracy; after ten years, statistics showed no appreciable increases in adult literacy in Latin America.

The Real Intention

Why was the Alliance for Progress such a failure? Before this question can be answered, a prior question must be asked: what was the real intention of those who created the Alliance? What purposes, and whose interests, was the Alliance designed to serve? On this question opinion has, for the most part, been divided into two camps. Liberal supporters have regarded the Alliance as a sincere effort to bring material progress and social justice to Latin America. Radical critics, on the other hand, have viewed it as simply a new tool for preventing revolution and protecting America's economic stake in Latin America. A noble experiment which foundered on the rock of Latin American realities, or an ideological fraud which in good measure succeeded in forestalling social change for yet another decade—these have been the terms in which most discussions of the Alliance have been couched.

While there is greater substance, in my opinion, in the argument of the critics, both sides have a hold on part of the truth about the Alliance for Progress. The Alliance goal of social change was genuine—as was its calculation of American self-interest. I shall treat the Alliance in each of these aspects—first as a failed "democratic revolution," then as a successful strategy for preserving the American economic empire in Latin America.

An Inherently Weak Theory

If we turn to writers who supported the Alliance, we find an interesting explanation proposed for the failure of Kennedy's "democratic revolution." Beyond the festering problems, bureaucratic inertia, and conservative resistance that hamstrung the Alliance, these writers stressed its incapacity to create a political "mystique" in Latin America. Despite the grand purposes and elevated language at its founding, the Alliance had come to seem just another aid program. As Tad Szulc, a *New York Times* journalist, put it,

... the concept of the Alliance somehow failed to electrify Latin America, contrary to what optimists in Washington had hoped and notwithstanding the early Latin American enthusiasm for the new Administration. Despite the noble and inspiring words of President Kennedy, the Alliance quickly proved to be virtually empty of the desperately needed political and psychological content. It was unable to project a mystique that would captivate the attention and the imagination of Latin Americans—as the Castro revolution had done in Cuba and in the rest of the Hemisphere.

That the Alliance for Progress failed to develop a mystique that inspired and involved the people of Latin America was true enough. But that failure could not, as these writers imagined, be attributed to an inattention to ideology or a paucity of public-relations efforts on the part of Washington. Though its backers did not realize it, the weakness of its political appeal was inherent in the basic theory of the Alliance itself.

If we examine the major premises of that theory closely, we can begin to see why it was bound to fail in Latin America. I shall consider four of these premises: (1) elitism and the fear of mass action (revolution from the top); (2) social change as manipulation by outside agencies (revolution from the outside); (3) maintenance of existing economic arrangements while "expanding the pie" for all (nondisruptive revolution); and (4) violence as the prerogative of the established order (nonviolent revolution). Each premise was essential to Kennedy's global liberalism. Each had its counterpart, too, in his domestic liberalism. The Alliance was to be an elaborate projection of the Kennedy Administration's pragmatic liberal faith—and a telling commentary on the illusions sustaining that faith. . . .

A Boon for Business

The Alliance for Progress, despite its noble pretensions, furthered American imperialism in Latin America. While most of its reforms failed to take hold, its efforts to maintain and increase American investments in the hemisphere were substantially successful. To some backers of the Alliance this outcome was no doubt satisfactory; their commitments had always been to the American corporate order in Latin America. In Kennedy's case, however, the Alliance was a profound disappointment. Kennedy was not a self-conscious or cynical imperialist. His motives were more complex; indeed, they were a prime source of the sort of contradictions that beset the Alliance from the outset.

Kennedy's relationship to the business community with regard to Latin America illustrated some of these contradictions. During the early days of the Alliance he spoke of putting the national interest of the United States (in Latin American development) above the interests of American corporations; further, he criticized the traditional idea that private investment was the panacea for Latin America's problems. In the Charter of Punta del Este encouragement of private enterprise was only one of the numerous goals—and it was overshadowed by the more dramatic reforms. But American business was not happy about being relegated to this secondary place in U.S. policy toward Latin America. Hence, [presidential adviser Arthur] Schlesinger reports, the Alliance came under "growing pressure from United States companies doing Latin American business to talk less about social reform and more about private investment."

As investment in Latin America lagged, Kennedy eventually succumbed to the pressure. References to the virtue of foreign investments now became more frequent in his speeches. By the time of his 1963 message to Congress on foreign aid, this had become a dominant theme: "The primary initiative in this year's program relates to our increased efforts to encourage the investment of private capital in the underdeveloped countries." Such capital was, he told the Inter-American Press Association on November 18, 1963, a key to the Alliance's eventual success: "If encouraged, private investment, responsive to the needs, the laws, and the interests of the nation, can cooperate with public activity to provide the vital margin of success as it did in the development of all the nations of the West. . . ."

. . . It was not business pressure, however, or business connections that ultimately made John Kennedy the servant of American imperialism in Latin America. A more crucial factor was his own ideological conviction. Kennedy saw himself, not as a tool of American corporations, but as a proponent of Latin American modernization. In the theory of modernization he had adopted, American investment was an aid to Latin American development; the profits flowing back to the United States were matched by the Latin Americans' profit in obtaining a modern industrial base. The protection and extension of the American economic stake in the hemisphere benefited all concerned. Kennedy thus was ill equipped to notice the contradictions: capital flowing out of Latin America faster than it flowed in, American corporations "developing" Latin America by exploiting its resources and subordinating its economic needs to their own, "nationalistic" and "progressive" bourgeoisie who collaborated with American corporate allies in maintaining a stagnant status quo. For all his analysis of Latin America's problems, Kennedy never grasped what was the single greatest roadblock to its progress—American imperialism.

Kennedy's goals in Latin America—material progress linked with reform, military suppression of revolutionary activity, protection of American property holdings—were, in his mind, fully consistent and congruent. But the first did not materialize; the record for the second was mixed; only the last was effectively accomplished. Reform and growth could not coexist in Latin America with repression and imperialist exploitation. Whatever generous and liberating impulses Kennedy's mode of global liberalism possessed were, therefore, inevitably subordinated in Latin America to its more selfish and repressive aims.

The Peace Corps Harnessed the Potential of Young Americans

Irving Bernstein

When he entered office, Kennedy did not have a formal plan in mind for what would become the Peace Corps. Yet, he sincerely wanted the United States to engage with the underdeveloped nations of the world in ways different from the strategic and economic policies of the Eisenhower administration. The day after his inauguration, Kennedy turned to several trusted advisers and asked them to develop the program that would become the Peace Corps. The president carefully ensured that the new program would be very different from other federal agencies. Irving Bernstein is an emeritus professor of political science at the University of California and the author of several noted books on the Great Depression.

J OHN KENNEDY WAS 43 WHEN HE BECAME PRESIDENT OF the United States. He was the youngest man ever to be elected to that office. Many thought it significant that he was the first President to have been born in the twentieth century (not especially early—1917), that this somehow symbolized a generational changing of the guard. Moreover, unlike those who look older than they are, Kennedy

Irving Bernstein, *Promises Kept: John F. Kennedy's New Frontier*. New York: Oxford University Press, 1991. Copyright © 1991 by Irving Bernstein. All rights reserved. Reproduced by permission of the publisher.

retained a boyish aspect. He enjoyed making little jokes about his youth, like riding up in a Capitol elevator and being asked by another passenger to let him off at the fourth floor. His age was both a liability and an asset. . . .

But youth also had political advantages. Kennedy drew great numbers of enthusiastic young people to his large campaign rallies. He was especially effective with college audiences, no more so than at 2:00 A.M. on October 14, 1960, at the Student Union at the University of Michigan, where he introduced the Peace Corps concept into his campaign. This led to the major address on that question at the Cow Palace in San Francisco on November 2, 1960. There was a chemistry at work: Kennedy's youth and the youth of America touched hands in the Peace Corps.

Ask Not . . .

At a planning session in Hyannis Port immediately after his election, Kennedy asked Sargent Shriver, his brother-in-law, to run a talent search for "the brightest and the best" people to staff the new administration. Shriver recruited Harris Wofford, Adam Yarmolinsky, and Louis Martin for his team. Buoyed by his unflagging example and leadership, they worked furiously at scouring the country for able people. This was the most exhaustive and productive search ever undertaken by a President-elect. If Kennedy had any doubts about Shriver's competence, this performance laid them to rest. . . .

In his inaugural address the next day the new President declared:

> To those people in the huts and villages of half the globe struggling to break the bonds of mass misery, we pledge our best efforts to help them help themselves, for whatever period is required—not because the communists may be doing it, not because we seek their votes, but because it is right. If a free society cannot help the many who are poor it cannot save the few who are rich. . . .

My fellow citizens of the world: ask not what America will do for you, but what together we can do for the freedom of man.

On January 21, evidently, Kennedy asked a bone-tired Shriver to make a study of how a Peace Corps could be organized. . . .

The Peace Corps

Kennedy was impatient to receive Shriver's report and inquired several times. A task force team wrote it under forced draft, with Wofford doing the final version. It arrived at the White House on February 24, 1961.

As for a Peace Corps, Shriver opened, "I recommend its immediate establishment." After having studied all the reports and consulting with many experts, he was satisfied that "we have sufficient answers to justify your going ahead." He then outlined the organization he thought would work.

Peace Corps volunteers would go abroad not as members of an official U.S. mission; rather, they would "go to teach, or to build, or to work in the communities to which they are sent." They would live with "the people they are helping." . . .

The corps would engage in a variety of activities and, therefore, "must have great flexibility to experiment with different methods of operation." Shriver did not want to see "a large centralized new bureaucracy." Thus, there must be an emphasis on farming out programs to private agencies, to universities, to other U.S. government agencies, and to the United Nations. But the Peace Corps would have to administer many projects itself, particularly in the teaching and large-scale construction areas.

Shriver visualized a nationwide recruitment program. "A simple announcement that Peace Corps application forms are available at all post offices . . . would probably produce an initial flood." It was critical that volunteers must be "the best available talent." Thus, recruitment, including testing, must be rigorous. "Widespread competition for Peace Corps positions with such careful screening is essential if people with the best chance of success are to be sent abroad."

Those selected must receive special training, which could range from six weeks to six months. This would include language instruction, preparation for the work assigned, and the problems of health and survival in the destination country.

The term of service must be at least one year, preferably two, and in some cases three or more. Volunteers must be subject to dismissal from the corps at any time during their service. There should be no top age limit for admission and both men and women should be welcomed. "In general corpsmen should be single"; the Peace Corps could not pay for a wife or children. Since Nixon had attacked the Peace Corps idea as "a haven for draft dodgers," Shriver wrote, "there should be no automatic draft exemption because of Peace Corps service." Nor should it be a "special domain of conscientious objectors." The pay should be "just enough to provide a minimum decent standard of living." Volunteers "should live in modest circumstances, and as closely as possible to their host country counterparts." . . .

Executive Order 10924

The timing of the launch, Shriver wrote, was critical. It could either await the passage of legislation, which could take many months, or it could be started by executive order within two weeks. If the former, summer 1961 training at universities would be lost and the year would be wasted. If the President acted now and the Peace Corps was financed by the transfer of available funds under the Mutual Security Act, it could have 1000 to 2000 volunteers overseas by the end of the year. This suggested a stress on teaching projects in the first year.

For a week there was a sharp debate between Shriver

and Sorensen. The latter was concerned that the Peace Corps might become a political liability and was especially disturbed that an executive order might anger Congress. Wiggins argued that, if Kennedy delayed, there might never be a Peace Corps. Josephson pointed out that FDR had established the Civilian Conservation Corps, a roughly parallel agency, by executive action.

On March 1, 1961, only a week after receiving Shriver's report, Kennedy compromised this disagreement both by issuing Executive Order 10924 establishing the Peace Corps on "a temporary basis" and by sending a special message to Congress asking for legislation for a permanent program....

When he became director of the Peace Corps, Shriver was forty-five, athletic, trim, and brimming with energy. He was extremely handsome, exceptionally personable, and unusually good at dealing with people. Brent Ashabranner called him a "glittering man." He had a wide range of friends and acquaintances. The Peace Corps mission appealed to all his impulses. "If the Peace Corps was to be a vehicle for American idealism," [Kennedy adviser] Arthur M. Schlesinger, Jr., wrote, "Shriver was an authentic and energetic idealist, well qualified to inspire both staff and volunteers with a sense of purpose and opportunity."

Shriver set to work furiously organizing the new agency. He took office space on the sixth floor of the [International Cooperation Association's] Maiataco Building on Connecticut Avenue and at the nearby Rochambeau Hotel....

Shriver imparted a particular style to the Peace Corps which made it unique among federal agencies. Robert G. Carey summed it up this way:

> There is little about the Peace Corps that is either standardized or scientific. It is an agency nearly devoid of artificial and calculated orthodoxy. The Corps has a litany, to be sure, but it is the litany of the explorer and frontiersman, not the organization man.

Challenges

In the spring of 1961 the fledgling Peace Corps faced a grave crisis. In March, Kennedy, in order to coordinate U.S. economic and social development programs, proposed that ICA, the Development Loan Fund, and Food for Peace be consolidated into a new umbrella organization to be called the Agency for International Development (AID). From the viewpoint of bureaucratic tidiness it was logical to put the Peace Corps into AID. . . .

Shriver and his staff were horrified because they thought the Peace Corps had a unique role to play and must be separated from the usual channels of American foreign policy. Shriver wrote a strong protest, but on March 30 Kennedy told him that Henry Labouisse [head of ICA] was heading a task force and he expected Shriver's full cooperation. The final meeting was scheduled for April 26. The timing was terrible because Shriver was going abroad four days earlier to persuade potential host countries to accept Peace Corps missions. In the meantime he lobbied Labouisse, Sorensen, and [Kennedy aide Ralph] Dungan, but to no avail. In fact, Kennedy was unable to attend the April 26 meeting because he was dealing with the Bay of Pigs disaster. Dungan was in the chair and steered the decision to incorporate the Peace Corps into AID. Kennedy later approved.

Shriver was in India when he learned the bad news. He felt "helpless" and feared that "the Peace Corps was about to die a-borning." All he could think of was to cable Wiggins to ask the Vice President to intercede. Wiggins sent Moyers, who played on LBJ's nostalgia over his New Deal experience in running the National Youth Administration in Texas and stressed his early support for the Peace Corps concept. Johnson responded immediately. "You put the Peace Corps into the foreign service and they'll put striped pants on your people when all you want them to have is a knapsack and a tool kit and a lot of imagination." He went to see the

President on May 1, and, as Josephson put it, "Johnson collared Kennedy . . . and . . . badgered him so much that Kennedy finally said all right." While this soured Shriver's relationship with the White House staff, it was a crucial decision to preserve the independence of the Peace Corps.

On April 22, 1961, Shriver had left with Wofford and several others for a twenty-six day trip to Ghana, Nigeria, Pakistan, India, Burma, Malaysia, Thailand, and the Philippines. It was a critical mission because no Third World nation had yet asked for Peace Corps assistance. There was widespread suspicion of American foreign policy, fear that the Peace Corps was a cover for CIA infiltration, and skepticism over the ability of rich young Americans to do any good in poverty-stricken villages. The Bay of Pigs misadventure was no help.

The skeptics underestimated Shriver. He returned with invitations from all eight countries he had visited for a total of 3000 volunteers. This opened the floodgates. A few days later Kennedy announced more than two dozen requests for aid. . . .

Working for Peace

The launching of the Peace Corps was an exceptionally complex operation. Broadly speaking, it involved the following: the creation of a headquarters staff and the writing of rules; the recruitment and training of volunteers; making contracts with host countries, which included not only acceptance of a Peace Corps mission but also determining what volunteers would do and arranging for their housing, travel, health, and a multitude of other matters; and developing, monitoring, and evaluating the programs. . . .

One of the main tasks at the outset was to lay down policies for the people in the field. Volunteers would live simply and unostentatiously, approximately at the level of the people they served. They must not match the standards of American diplomatic and AID personnel abroad. They would not be paid salaries, merely subsistence. Each would bank $75 for each month of service, payable as a termination allowance. He or she would also earn leave time at the rate of two and one-half days for each month served. But leaves must be taken in the Third not the First World. . . .

The Peace Corps adopted a policy of nondiscrimination, including what would later be called affirmative action, in the recruitment of blacks, Latinos, and other minorities. This was based in part on the sensible premise that overseas programs would be overwhelmingly in nonwhite nations and that Americans who were not Caucasians would fit in more easily. Muslim countries, excepting Tunisia and Morocco later on, did not get contracts because they refused to accept Jewish volunteers. Universities in the South were not offered training programs because they declined to admit Negroes. Despite the policy of nondiscrimination, the number of black volunteers between 1961 and 1963 never exceeded 5 percent. This was because there were very few Negro college graduates and most of them preferred paying jobs at home. Women were also welcomed and by 1963 constituted about 40 percent of the 7000 volunteers.

The Peace Corps considered the selection process to be critical, that it was preferable to avoid a mistake early than to suffer from it later. Thus, the weeding-out process was rigorous. The applicant had to answer a comprehensive twelve-page questionnaire, submit six references, take a six-hour written examination, and submit to a thorough medical checkup, followed by psychiatric observation. It was difficult to pass through all these gates. Moritz Thomsen, a forty-eight-year-old farmer from Red Bluff, California, wrote that "we were studied and appraised like a bunch of fat beeves about to be entered in the state fair."

In March 1961, even before forms had been distributed to post offices, the Peace Corps received 10,000 letters from potential applicants. When the forms went out Shriver expected 15,000 completed applications, but received only half that number. Only 3500 took the first examination on May 27. The assumption that recruitment would take care of itself did not work out. Shriver then threw himself into a high-pressure drive, including TV and radio advertising, and by mid-year had 10,000 applicants. In 1962 there were 20,000, and in 1963 almost 35,000. This raised internal concern over whether quality was being sacrificed for big numbers.

The Peace Corps developed a three-phase training program: eight to ten weeks at a U.S. university (usually in the summer when professors, classrooms, and dormitories were available); two to four weeks at a Peace Corps outdoor camp in Puerto Rico, Hawaii, St. Croix, or St. Thomas; and one to two weeks in the host country.

The universities provided an eight-course core program: skills for jobs to be performed overseas; language, with a stress on conversation; area studies; world affairs, including the danger of Communist subversion; American studies; physical education; health care; and orientation on the Peace Corps.

Those who completed the training thought that they had suffered through boot camp. Thomsen took his at Montana State in Bozeman. "Peace Corps training," he wrote, "is like no other training in the world, having something in common with college life, officer's training, Marine basic training, and a ninety-day jail sentence." The typical university schedule was 7:00 A.M. to 10:00 P.M. six days a week. There were special supplements. Volunteers bound for the slums of Colombian cities did time in Spanish Harlem, those going to Nepal climbed the Rockies. The outdoor camps were even tougher: calisthenics at 5:00 A.M. and a ten-hour day six days a week. The American public ate it up. As Gerard Rice wrote, "Reporters filed into Peace Corps' field camps to see trainees swinging through trees, scaling sheer cliffs, and being thrown into rivers bound hand and foot (presumably the sort of tests that would await them in the jungles of the Third World!).". . .

A Legacy

From the moment of its inception the Peace Corps became extraordinarily popular. Ashabranner spoke of "America's love affair with the Peace Corps." In part this was due to Shriver and his unusual gift for public relations. . . .

But the popularity was due to more than its director. As David Hapgood pointed out, "millions of Americans . . . want to believe that their country is capable of doing *something* good overseas and have therefore invested the Peace Corps with a degree of magic, self-sacrifice and piety. . . ." This was an exaggeration, but it had a large kernel of truth. The agency suffered from no scandal. It enjoyed a favored position with the media. Congress looked on it with great favor and gave it more money than Shriver could use.

The Peace Corps' popularity also stemmed from its style. It seemed to be everything that Americans did not expect a government agency to be. It was youthful, brash, courageous, tough, innovative, informal, hard-working, and anti-bureaucratic. Josephson prevented the publication of an organization manual because he thought it would be "stultifying." Ashabranner wrote that most of the volunteers he knew were "strong-minded, strong-willed, high-spirited men and women, suspicious of anything that looked even remotely like a restraining bureaucracy.". . .

The effectiveness of the Peace Corps to the nations of the Third World must be viewed in the proper focus. This was a micro- rather than a macro-program. Thus, it did not bring peace to the world or to its regions. Nor did it stimulate economic development on more than a minuscule scale. Nor did it become an instrument of American foreign policy. . . .

The accomplishments were on a small scale. The Peace Corps taught mothers how to keep themselves and their children clean in order to avoid disease. It helped provide public sanitation with water systems and sewage disposal. It taught people to read and write and do sums. It showed farmers how to produce healthy crops, poultry, and farm animals. It planned and helped build roads to give remote villages access to the outside world. It assisted in administering birth control programs. Perhaps most important, it gave extremely poor and forgotten people the sense that they mattered.

Kennedy Revolutionized U.S. Food Aid Policy

Mitchel B. Wallerstein

During his presidential campaign, Kennedy promised to transform U.S. agricultural policies by using surplus crops grown in the United States to improve America's relations with countries. Specifically, Kennedy wanted to expand the existing Food for Peace Program (known as PL 480) and integrate U.S. efforts with broader multinational programs, including those administered by the United Nations. The president astutely realized that the Food for Peace program was one method to operationalize his campaign theme of "the New Frontier."

Mitchel B. Wallerstein is the vice president for the Program on Global Security and Sustainability of the John D. and Catherine T. MacArthur Foundation. In this overview of Kennedy's Food for Peace program, Wallerstein contends that the young president dramatically changed U.S. food aid policy from being primarily a domestic-focused program to help U.S. farmers dispose of surplus crops into a true attempt to alleviate famine in hunger in the world.

FROM THE EARLY DAYS OF THE 1960 CAMPAIGN, IT WAS APparent that John F. Kennedy was far more attuned to the use of food in international relations than he was to the

Mitchel B. Wallerstein, *Food for War—Food for Peace: United States Food Aid in a Global Context.* Cambridge, MA: MIT Press, 1980. Copyright © 1980 by The Massachusetts Institute of Technology. All rights reserved. Reproduced by permission of The MIT Press, Cambridge, MA.

needs or problems of domestic agriculture. While agricultural speeches tended to bore both the candidate and his audiences, Kennedy was able to speak at length extemporaneously about his plans for the use of American food aid. For example, during a campaign swing through South Dakota, Kennedy stated,

> I don't regard the existence of . . . agricultural surpluses as a problem. I regard it as an opportunity. . . . I think the farmers can bring more credit, more lasting good will, more chance for peace, than almost any other group of Americans in the next ten years, if we recognize that food is strength, and food is peace and food is freedom, and food is a helping hand to people around the world whose good will and friendship we want.

Also during the campaign, Kennedy announced the appointment of a "committee of distinguished citizens" to formulate recommendations for his new administration "to transfer the 'food for peace' slogan into a truly effective long-range use of our food abundance."

The candidate proposed a six-point program designed to transform the slogan into action:

1. Change the surplus emphasis of the program into the use of food as a "long-range investment in progress."
2. Centralize responsibility for all phases of overseas distribution of US foods.
3. Increase substantially the annual amount of food and fiber to be distributed overseas by the voluntary relief agencies.
4. Continue and improve government-to-government assistance in the case of sudden disasters.
5. Hold a second International Conference on Food and Agriculture, similar to the one convened at Hot Springs, Virginia by Franklin Roosevelt, "to deal on

a constructive multilateral basis with the food needs of the world."

6. Pending such a conference and creation of "a world food agency," negotiate long-term agreements for donor countries to supply food commodities for food-for-work schemes.

It seems reasonable to suggest on the basis of this evidence that the new President *was* committed to a fundamental change in the objectives of US food policy and in the manner in which the aid was distributed.

A New Food Aid Policy

After his inauguration, Kennedy moved swiftly to implement his new conception of food aid policy by establishing the Office of Food for Peace within the Executive Office of the President and by naming his friend and campaign supporter, George McGovern, as it first director. The concept of food aid seemed well suited to Kennedy's New Frontier image, with its emphasis on social and technological optimism. This optimism was characterized by the belief that all problems were solvable with the appropriate combination of money, technology, and expertise.

The food aid policy of the new Secretary of Agriculture, Orville Freeman, was even a step ahead of the President's own conception. The Secretary of Agriculture, who was to become the linchpin of subsequent efforts under Kennedy to expand the developmental impact of Food for Peace, urged the President to formalize the US commitment to *eradicate* (not simply relieve) worldwide malnutrition by submitting to the Congress a USDA evaluation of the total resources required and then by making a "very bold statement in connection with the percentage of the deficiency that we as a nation are willing to meet." Freeman proposed that we would then go about producing the things needed to meet that deficiency. A policy of consciously planned production was indeed a radical departure from the surplus disposal mentality of the previous decade, requiring that food aid be allocated henceforth on the basis of recipient need rather than simply as a result of commodity availability.

Freeman marshaled three arguments favoring such a fundamental alteration of US policy. First, it would be consistent with the traditional US philosophy and policy of sharing its agricultural abundance. Second, it would represent a great and dramatic step which would bring to the attention of the world the fact that the United States was no longer dumping its surpluses willy-nilly, but was instead producing food for human use.... Finally, it would be part of a long-term effort to expand markets for the product of US agriculture....

Other foreign policy initiatives involving food aid were also emerging from the White House in 1961–1962. For example, at the behest of George McGovern, Kennedy approved US participation in the three-year experimental multilateral food aid undertaking which eventually became the UN-FAO World Food Programme....

Food Aid as Foreign Policy

Claims to the specific authorship of the "Food for Peace" slogan for the PL 480 program are numerous, but the evidence would seem to support attribution to the late Senator Hubert H. Humphrey. Whoever the originator, the idea was soon coopted by the Eisenhower administration and a Food for Peace Coordinator was appointed in 1960. But the evidence also indicates that the Republican initiative was primarily an effort to repackage old programs under a new name in order to preempt the Democrats in an election year.

Presidential candidate John F. Kennedy and his campaign staff had a different vision of the program, however. They viewed it more in terms of its potential as an instrument of foreign policy than as a pressure release valve for farm surpluses. Moreover, the Kennedy people considered the issue of food aid to be an ideal element of their innovative New Frontier image. They believed that if the Democratic candidate could be associated in the voters' minds with solid, humanitarian causes like food assistance, it would serve both to improve his election chances and to promote the development of bold new programmatic thrusts once in office. Candidate Kennedy therefore announced in October 1960 the appointment of a "committee of distinguished citizens" to formulate recommendations on how the new administration might transfer the Food for Peace slogan into "a truly effective long-range use of our food abundance to build foundations for durable peace and progress."

In their report to the then President-elect on 19 January 1961, the committee recommended, among other things, that "to insure that the program functions vigorously, it is necessary to have a central point of responsibility and initiative (i.e., an Office of Food for Peace) . . . and an officer (i.e., a Food for Peace Director) . . . to be responsible to the President and serve as his principal adviser and agent in connection with the Food for Peace program." This advice paralleled closely the recommendations of a number of other Kennedy staffers including Arthur M. Schlesinger, Jr., who also recognized the political and public relations potential of such a high-visibility program coordinated at the White House level. Consequently, by executive order (the second such directive of his presidency), Kennedy established the position of Director of Food for Peace and directed that the Office of Food for Peace (OFFP) be located within the Executive Office of the President. But the President also had a secondary reason for his decision that was related far more to partisan political concerns.

The Food Aid Program Takes Shape

John Kennedy decided to appoint George McGovern as the Director of the Office for Food for Peace, promising him enhanced responsibility and a high degree of public visibility in preparation for a second campaign bid.

McGovern seemed tailor made for the position, possessing both a strong concern for agriculture and a deep feeling for the humanitarian aspect of the world hunger problem. The task as set out by Kennedy also needed doing since the Food for Peace concept had never actually been implemented under Eisenhower, due to the lack of political commitment and to interagency jealousies. McGovern was charged specifically with eliminating these bottlenecks. He became both coordinator and expediter, not administering the food aid program in an operational sense but acting as the focal point within the administration for all food aid–related issues and discussions.

The object of his efforts was to modify the operational focus of the PL 480 program in order to reflect the new approach to foreign aid then being developed within the administration and to mobilize public opinion in support of food aid and in economic assistance in general. In order to pursue the public relations aspect, an American Food for Peace Council was created by Presidential invitation in June 1961. Over one hundred representatives from agriculture, labor, industry, commerce, and civic groups were invited to participate. The council was requested to develop public information on world hunger, to enlist public support for the "attack" on world hunger, and to advise the Food for Peace director. McGovern also initiated additional promotional efforts early in 1962 by enlisting the services of the US Advertising Council to mount a public information campaign—similar in many respects to that undertaken on behalf of the newly established Peace Corps—to raise the level of citizen awareness concerning the humanitarian and *ideological* importance of food aid.

Freedom from Hunger

As expected, George McGovern announced his resignation as Director of Food for Peace in July 1962 in order to run once again for a Senate seat from South Dakota. He was replaced by Richard Reuter, then President of CARE, Inc., and the White House was careful to emphasize its desire to take "no action that would seem to downgrade the Food for Peace function [of] Mr. McGovern's service as Director of Food for Peace or in any way impair his chances in the fall election. The President's deep personal interest in Food for Peace must be clearly recognized." Kennedy did, in fact, continue to maintain an interest in the food aid program, and he ordered Reuter to mount a major effort to end the interagency squabbling over the PL 480 program and to shift thinking at the operational level from surplus disposal philosophy to a recognition of the political and economic value of food aid.

Reuter also undertook to make good on the Kennedy campaign pledge to convene an international food conference commemorating the twentieth anniversary of the FAO. The proposal for a World Food Congress was approved by the President in October 1962 and the meeting was scheduled for June 1963. Over twelve hundred international participants were invited, including private citizens, academicians, representatives of nongovernmental organizations, and the like.

From the White House perspective, convening such a conference fulfilled a number of the administration's goals and interests simultaneously. First, it made good on the Kennedy campaign pledge, and it emphasized the President's *personal* interest and commitment to the problem of world hunger. Second, it focused international attention of the problems of hunger and population and emphasized the need for coordinated global action. John Kennedy personally delivered the keynote address of the congress, and with typical rhetorical flourish, he underscored the importance of the hunger problem:

> For the first time in the history of the world we do know
> how to produce enough food now to feed every man,

woman and child in the world, enough to eliminate all hunger completely.

So long as freedom from hunger is only half achieved, so long as two-thirds of the nations have food deficits, no citizen, no nation, can afford to be satisfied. We have the ability, as members of the human race. We have the means, we have the capacity to eliminate hunger from the face of the earth in our lifetime. We need only the will.

It is interesting to speculate on the direction US food aid policy might have taken had John Kennedy lived to complete his first term and, perhaps, to serve for a second. But, five months after his World Food Congress speech, he was gone.

Successes of the Program

During its five-year existence, the OFFP had served a valuable *symbolic* function in demonstrating the personal commitment of the President to the problem of world hunger and malnutrition. This support came at a time when the use of food aid and all economic assistance as a foreign policy instrument was in a period of critical transition. The existence of the OFFP thus served to increase the public visibility of the PL 480 program, to further the political career of its first director, George McGovern, and to facilitate, at least to some degree, the coordination of agency efforts in the allocation of food aid.

CIVIL RIGHTS

Kennedy Balanced Practical Politics with Moral Leadership on Civil Rights

Charles Kenney

When Kennedy entered the White House, civil rights expectations were mixed, as many blacks hoped for swift action while politicians doubted the new president's commitment to the issue. Such dramatic events as the Bay of Pigs invasion and the Cuban missile crisis made it difficult for Kennedy to push a domestic agenda, and the president frequently found himself having to juggle competing issues while balancing demands from civil rights activists, southerners, and anticommunist hawks. This essay maintains that Kennedy managed to balance practical political realities with the need to use the presidency as a place of moral leadership. The author, Charles Kenney, is an historian at the John F. Kennedy Library and Museum in Boston.

CORETTA SCOTT KING FEARED HER HUSBAND WOULD BE murdered. When Martin Luther King Jr. was sentenced to six months hard labor for a traffic violation, Mrs. King believed he would tumble into the recesses of the Georgia state penal system never to come out alive. Her fears were shared by many American Negroes. Mrs. King

Charles Kenney, *John F. Kennedy: The Presidential Portfolio*. New York: Public Affairs Press, 2000. Copyright © 2000 by Charles Kenney. All rights reserved. Reproduced by permission of Sterling Lord Literistic, Inc.

was five months pregnant at the time, and though she had lived with the fright and peril of having a husband who was emerging as the most prominent civil rights advocate in the nation, this was the penal system of the state of Georgia. King's sentence came during the third week of October 1960, a mere two weeks before a presidential election that was expected to be tight and in which both parties were competing for the Negro vote. Some of Kennedy's campaign workers had been urging the candidate to make a gesture of some kind that would appeal to Negro voters. His brother-in-law Sargent Shriver suggested that Kennedy call Mrs. King and comfort her.

"Negroes don't expect everything will change tomorrow, no matter who's elected," said Shriver. "But they do want to know whether you care. If you telephone Mrs. King, they will know you understand and will help. You will reach their hearts and give support to a pregnant woman who's afraid her husband will be killed."

"Get her on the phone," Kennedy said, and Shriver did.

"I want to express to you my concern about your husband," Kennedy told Mrs. King. "I know this must be very hard for you. I understand you are expecting a baby and I just wanted you to know that I was thinking about you and Dr. King. If there is anything I can do to help, please feel free to call on me."

Mrs. King was deeply moved by the call, and she said so publicly. Her father-in-law, the Reverend Martin Luther King Sr., an influential voice among Negroes, switched from Nixon to Kennedy on the strength of that call alone. "I had expected to vote against Senator Kennedy because of his religion," said the senior King. "But now he can be my president, Catholic or whatever he is. It took courage to call my daughter-in-law at a time like this. He has the moral courage to stand up for what he knows is right. . . . I've got all my votes and I've got a suitcase and I'm going to take them up there and dump them in his lap." The Reverend Ralph David Abernathy, a leading civil rights activist, exulted over the call, saying that Kennedy had done "something great and wonderful."

Robert Kennedy was furious when he later heard about the call, for he feared it was a grave political miscalculation that could cost his brother votes in key southern states. But when word of the call reached the press, the reaction of Negroes was one of overwhelming support for JFK. (Seeing this, Robert Kennedy went so far as to call the judge in the case and ask for King's release.)

Dr. King himself, upon his triumphant release from prison, said, "I am deeply indebted to Senator Kennedy, who served as a great force in making my release possible. It took a lot of courage for Senator Kennedy to do this . . . for him to be that courageous shows that he is really acting upon principle and not expediency."

The call to Mrs. King would prove to be pivotal, for in the closest presidential election in history, Kennedy carried an overwhelming 70 percent of the Negro vote.

High Expectations

When John F. Kennedy entered the White House, the expectations for what he would accomplish on civil rights could hardly have been higher. Civil rights leaders expected the new president to deliver quickly on his campaign promise to eliminate discrimination in federally subsidized housing. They expected the president to support comprehensive civil rights legislation. They expected, in short, that Kennedy's actions would show that he was on their side, that their cause was his. His sympathies certainly lay with Negro Americans. He had been president for barely an hour when he watched the inaugural parade and bridled at the absence of any Negroes in the detachment marching from the Coast Guard Academy. "Call the commandant," the president snapped, "and tell him I don't ever want to see that happen again."

But when John F. Kennedy took the oath of office, he was almost entirely preoccupied with the danger of the world, with the Communist threat and the possibility of nuclear confrontation, with the very survival of the nation. No other issue—not civil rights, not taxes, not the economy generally—even came close to capturing Kennedy's time and attention.

Practical political considerations also played a critical role in the president's thinking on civil rights. Having served in both the House and Senate, Kennedy fully understood the political realities he faced. Though his own party held a sixty-five-to-thirty-five-seat majority in the Senate and a 263-to-174 majority in the House, he knew from experience that real congressional power lay with conservative southern committee chairmen in the Senate and a coalition of Republicans and southern Democrats in the House. While he was pushed hard and early by civil rights leaders to propose comprehensive civil rights legislation, Kennedy knew he needed the full support of key House and Senate members to pass legislation for a military buildup, for more weapons systems. The president had a general timetable in mind for civil rights: He would take some steps during his first term, but then, after a solid reelection, he would be in a position to make significant strides.

Patience

He also did not believe the country was quite ready for rapid change and did not want to be perceived among key southerners on Capitol Hill or among the American people as prematurely pushing a civil rights agenda. "First things first," said presidential confidant Theodore Sorensen in the early days of the administration. "He concentrates on what he has to concentrate on." And that meant the international situation, particularly Cuba, Berlin, Khrushchev, and the growing Communist threat. Civil rights leaders were sympathetic to the president's position.

They understood that the world was a dangerous place and knew that Kennedy had to focus a good deal of attention on the world stage. Still, they wanted progress, and when little came in the early days, they were frustrated. Very soon after the election, it became clear to Roy Wilkins, head of the NAACP and one of the most prominent civil rights leaders of the time, that "Kennedy had no intention of beginning his new administration with a full-scale legislative program for civil rights."

Kennedy urged patience. Kennedy Library records contain the blunt reply to the president from baseball great Jackie Robinson, a Republican then in private business. "I would like to be patient, Mr. President," Robinson wrote to Kennedy just a few weeks into the new administration, "but patience has [cost] us years in our struggle for human dignity." When leaders from the 1961 NAACP convention in Washington were invited to meet with the president in the White House, they asked that he propose and support comprehensive civil rights legislation. But the president said no. "We remain convinced that legislation is not the way," he said. "At least it is not advisable at this time."

Wilkins and other leaders were disappointed: "We wanted Congress and the White House to come out of hiding and line up alongside the Supreme Court on segregation. We thought we had had a clear promise from the Democrats and from Kennedy himself to do just that, but now he was backing down. We were off to a very bad start with Kennedy."

Balancing Issues

Rather than seeing it as "backing down," Kennedy viewed his caution on civil rights as entirely rational given the harsh political realities on Capitol Hill and with the cold war. Barely a month into office, Kennedy met with Father Theodore Hesburgh, then president of the University of Notre Dame and chairman of the U.S. Civil Rights Commission. Father Hesburgh pointed out to Kennedy that the Alabama National Guard was entirely segregated.

"Look, father," Kennedy said, "I may have to send the Alabama National Guard to Berlin tomorrow and I don't want to have to do it in the middle of a revolution at home."

By April Roy Wilkins was moved to write a personal note to Harris Wofford, a friend and Kennedy's adviser on civil rights. Wilkins recognized Kennedy's attention to the international situation: "We do have a difference with the Kennedy Administration and perhaps that difference is rooted in the purpose of the NAACP as contrasted with the purpose of the government of all the people in a time of world crisis." This was an important acknowledgment of the position the president was in. Nonetheless, Wilkins was frustrated. "The Kennedy Administration has done with Negro citizens what it has done with a vast number of Americans: it has charmed them. It has intrigued them. Every seventy-two hours it has delighted them. On the Negro question it has smoothed Unguentine on a stinging burn even though for a moment (or for perhaps a year) it cannot do anything about a broken pelvis."

Freedom Rides

Just a month before Kennedy took office, the U.S. Supreme Court ruled that segregation was illegal in facilities serving interstate travelers. As a result, segregation was banned in places such as bus terminal waiting rooms, bathrooms, and restaurants in terminals used by buses traveling interstate. The Freedom Riders challenged restrictions that remained in spite of the Supreme Court ruling. Interracial groups of Freedom Riders intended to travel via Trailways and Greyhound buses throughout the Deep South. "We propose to challenge, en route, every form of segregation met by the bus passenger," James Farmer of the Congress of Racial Equality (CORE), the Freedom Ride organizer, wrote to Kennedy. "We are experienced in, and dedicated to, the

Gandhian principles of non-violence."

The Freedom Riders departed Washington by bus on May 4, 1961. For ten days, they were merely anonymous travelers, but on May 14 they made news across America. On that day, as seven Freedom Riders traveled through Alabama, their bus was attacked. Farmer dispatched an urgent telegram to the president:

> Today a Greyhound bus travelling from Atlanta to Birmingham was ambushed outside of Anniston, Alabama, by fifty white men, its tires slashed, windows smashed, tear gas hurled inside and the bus finally set afire and gutted by flames....
>
> One hour later, seven other interstate freedom riders on a Trailways bus also at Anniston, Alabama, were severely beaten by eight hoodlums inside the bus after Negro passengers failed to move to rear seats when ordered to do so by the bus driver.... Arriving in Birmingham the CORE freedom riders were again attacked by a mob and at least one freedom rider hospitalized with severe cuts....

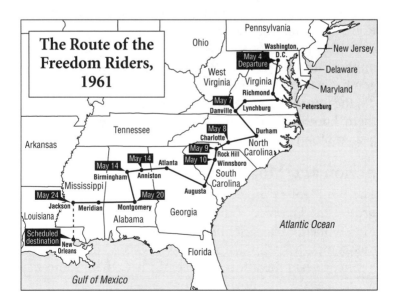

The Route of the Freedom Riders, 1961

Federal investigation and intervention urgently required. Equally imperative that moral force of your office be exerted. The president must speak.

Soon other Freedom Riders were attacked and beaten in Birmingham. Kennedy was angry about the Freedom Rides in part because he believed that the spectacle of violence against black Americans embarrassed the nation before the world. Kennedy asked his civil rights adviser, Harris Wofford, "Can't you get your goddamned friends off those buses? Stop them." The president believed that the disruption caused by the Freedom Riders in the South would make it more difficult for him to deal with key southerners in the Congress. Robert Kennedy agreed with his brother, saying to Wofford, "I wonder whether [the Freedom Riders] have the best interest of their country at heart. . . . The president is going abroad and this is all embarrassing him." A May Gallup Poll showed that nearly two-thirds of all Americans disapproved of the Freedom Riders.

Kennedy nonetheless recognized that the Freedom Riders had the law of the land squarely on their side. The president assigned his most trusted adviser, his brother Robert, to monitor the situation closely. Robert Kennedy sent his administrative assistant, John Seigenthaler, the only southerner in his office, to Birmingham. When Seigenthaler asked Robert Kennedy what he wanted him to do, the attorney general replied: "Hold their hands and let them know we care." In Montgomery, Seigenthaler was beaten bloody and unconscious.

Action and Moral Leadership

The president responded by dispatching U.S. marshals to protect the Freedom Riders. When a Freedom Riders' bus was stopped, Robert Kennedy telephoned an official at the bus company in Birmingham. "Mr. Cruit, this is Robert Kennedy," said the attorney general. "Isn't there some way we can get this bus down to Montgomery?"

"No, sir," Cruit said, adding that the drivers were fearful for their lives and "refused to drive."

"Do you have anybody else that can drive this bus?" Kennedy asked. "Any other driver."

"No," said Cruit.

Kennedy was angry.

"Mr. Cruit," he said, "I think if I were you I would get a driver of one of the colored buses and have them take the bus down. You can get one of them, can't you?"

"No," replied Cruit.

"Well, hell, you can look for one, can't you? After all, these people have tickets and are entitled to transportation to continue the trip . . . to Montgomery."

But Cruit persisted in saying that there were no drivers available.

"Do you know how to drive a bus?" Kennedy asked.

"No," said Cruit.

"Well, surely somebody in the damn bus company can drive a bus, can't they?"

When Cruit still would not budge, Kennedy said: "Mr. Cruit, I think you . . . had better be getting in touch with Mr. Greyhound or whoever Greyhound is. . . . I am—the government—is going to be very much upset if this group does not get to continue their trip. . . . Somebody better get in the damn bus and get it going and get these people on their way."

While the Freedom Riders were continuing their challenge down South, Kennedy met at the White House with a group of people involved with the Peace Corps, including Harry Belafonte, a popular black entertainer, who asked the president to be more outspoken in support of the Freedom Riders. During the same meeting, Eugene Rostow, the dean of Yale Law School, looked at the president and flatly said: "There is a need now for moral leadership." This angered Kennedy. "Have you read my statement in the newspapers?" Kennedy replied.

The president was feeling put upon. Here he was getting ready for one of the most important meetings of his life—his Vienna summit with Khrushchev was just weeks away—and he was being hectored at home. When the group had left, Kennedy vented his anger on Wofford. "What in the world does he think I should do?" Kennedy asked. "Doesn't he know I've done more for civil rights than any president in American history? How could any man have done more than I've done?"

Toward the end of the president's first year in office, civil rights leaders were growing increasingly impatient with what they perceived to be the president's unwillingness to follow through on his campaign promise to abolish discrimination in federally funded housing "with the stroke of a pen." A campaign mocking the president's promise had already begun, and thousands of pens were mailed to the White House in protest. In November 1961 some civil rights leaders left a White House meeting with Kennedy carrying the clear impression that the order was on the eve of being issued. In mid-December, when the order was not forthcoming, Roy Wilkins sent a frankly worded telegram to the president:

> Grave concern and considerable skepticism and some resentment have arisen across the country since the November 27 announcement that an agreed-upon draft was ready of an order prohibiting racial discrimination in federally assisted housing. There is real fear that unless it is issued at this time it may not be issued. The millions whose high hopes were encouraged by the clear commitment of the administration feel that the redemption of a 1960 promise should not rest upon anticipated developments in 1962.

Kennedy and King

If the criticism from Wilkins was bad, there was more to come. In March 1962 Martin Luther King Jr. offered his assessment of Kennedy in an article in the *Nation* titled "Report on Civil Rights; Fumbling on the New Frontier." According to King:

> The Kennedy administration in 1961 waged an essentially cautious and defensive struggle for civil rights. . . . As the year unfolded, Executive initiative became increasingly feeble, and the chilling prospect emerged of a general Administration retreat. In backing away from an executive order to end discrimination in housing, the President did more to undermine confidence in his intentions than could be offset by a series of smaller accomplishments during the year. He has begun 1962 with a show of renewed aggressiveness; one can only hope that it will be sustained.

> The year 1961 was characterized by inadequacy and incompleteness in [civil rights]. . . . It is not only that the Administration too often retreated in haste from a battlefield which it has proclaimed a field of honor, but— more significantly—its basic strategic goals have been narrowed.

Kennedy nonetheless stayed his cautious course. He continued to express frustration that he was being pushed too hard on civil rights and that the country wasn't ready for action that overreached. Kennedy felt he knew the Hill well enough to know that the perception that he was being overly aggressive with a civil rights agenda could badly harm his ability to work with congressional leaders. When members of the U.S. Civil Rights Commission told him that it intended to open public hearings on complaints of racial discrimination in Mississippi, Kennedy asked the commission not to proceed. "You're making my life difficult," the president said to the chairman.

The president expressed his frustration one day to Louis Martin, the publisher of a chain of Negro newspapers in Chicago and the president's single Negro adviser. "Negroes are getting ideas they didn't have before," Martin told the president.

"Where are they getting them?" the president asked.

"From you!" Martin replied. "You're lifting the horizons of Negroes!"

Kennedy Missed Opportunities to Act Forcefully on Civil Rights

Donald W. Jackson and James W. Riddlesperger Jr.

Even though Kennedy is generally given credit for promoting civil rights, authors Donald W. Jackson and James W. Riddlesperger Jr. weigh the evidence from presidential records and statements and suggest otherwise. Kennedy inherited the sensitive and important crisis of the rights of blacks in the U.S. South. Although he appointed a civil rights commission, the authors argue that his deeds did not match his rhetoric and Kennedy missed opportunities to act forcefully to promote civil rights. A former attorney and judicial fellow at the Supreme Court, Jackson is a professor of political science at Texas Christian University who has written several books on the law, policy, and equality. Riddlesperger is also a professor at TCU who publishes widely on the presidency.

BY ALL ACCOUNTS, KENNEDY HAD ONLY PASSING INTEREST in civil rights politics before running for president. [Kennedy's special counsel Ted] Sorensen writes that in his pre-presidential days, Kennedy "knew and cared relatively little about the problems of civil rights and civil liberties."

Donald W. Jackson and James W. Riddlesperger Jr., *Presidential Leadership and Civil Rights Policy*. Westport, CT: Greenwood Press, 1995. Copyright © 1995 by the Policy Studies Organization. All rights reserved. Reproduced by permission of the publisher.

On the most important issue that confronted Kennedy while in Congress, the Civil Rights Act of 1957, Kennedy acted pragmatically. In the abstract sense, he was committed to a strong civil rights measure, advocating the strongest section of the bill, which would have granted the Justice Department strong enforcement powers. That section was omitted from the bill by Senate vote. The most controversial section of the bill, which gave those accused of violating the Civil Rights Act the right to have a jury trial (which in the South might have severely limited the impact of the bill), was one that the strongest advocates of civil rights opposed. Kennedy supported the amendment after determining that the provision would probably not have much impact and that the bill could not pass without it.

With the Stroke of a Pen?

During the 1960 campaign, Kennedy did two things which attracted great attention: he argued that the executive powers of the president could outlaw discrimination in federally subsidized housing and in businesses that held government contracts "with the stroke of a pen," and he made the phone call to Coretta Scott King on the eve of the election. Both have been cited as illustrations of the Kennedy commitment to civil rights, and yet each has a pragmatic turn. The "stroke of a pen" comment has an interesting history of its own. [Kennedy adviser Richard] Goodwin suggests that he wrote it for delivery in a campaign speech, and that Kennedy delivered the line "without the slightest hint of doubt or equivocation." [Adviser Harris] Wofford remembers that he had used the phase in his own speeches and that Kennedy adopted it in one of the debates with Richard Nixon. Whatever the origin of the phrase, it became an albatross for Kennedy by 1962. Civil rights activists were beginning to exert constant pressure, encouraging their supporters to send JFK a pen, since his apparently was dry. Pens came to the White House by the thousands. Kennedy was concerned that the timing was wrong and that an executive order might delay other items on his legislative agenda. It led him to query in frustration, "Who the hell wrote that?" While Kennedy had a commitment to act, he did not want to be forced to act before he thought it tactically advantageous.

The phone call to Coretta King also needs interpretation. No record exists that Kennedy ever explained his motivation for the call. Stern argues that the call was not a planned-out, strategic move by the candidate. Instead, it was planned by Harris Wofford and [director of the Peace Corps] Sargent Shriver to be done on the spur of the moment. They wanted the candidate to call her both because they were concerned and because they believed that neither the candidate nor the rest of the campaign staff understood the black voters' intensity and depth of concern with the issue. Perhaps Martin Luther King, Jr. summarized it best in saying that "there are moments in history . . . that what is morally right is politically expedient, politically sound. And I would like to feel—I really feel this— that he made the call because he was concerned. He had come to know me as a person. . . . At the same time, I think he naturally had political considerations in mind."

Quickly and Quietly

Kennedy wished to deal with civil rights quickly and quietly, so that it might not interfere with other priorities. In August 1960, he asked Harris Wofford, "Now in five minutes, tick off the things a President ought to do to clean up this goddamn civil rights mess." Once elected, Kennedy wished to develop a political strategy to deal with the civil right issues. He had Harris Wofford prepare a memo outlining a plan. Wofford's thirty-one-page memo proposed "little or no legislation this year aside from the extension of the Civil Rights Commission, and a large measure of executive action. You have the power to do more than you will be able to do on this problem in one year. If you make this a year full of executive action you can overcome the disappointment of Negroes and civil rights groups, although they will holler for a while." This important memo shows that even among the strongest administration advocates of civil rights reform there was a feeling that pushing too fast on legislation might limit the effectiveness of Kennedy's overall program. Instead, it recommended that the president take a personal interest in executive action. The record shows that while a great deal of executive action occurred, it was largely done by Kennedy's subordinates, mostly in the Justice Department, and was done as quietly as could be, in as conciliatory a manner as possible. Ken-

A Moral Crisis

Michael A. Genovese, the author of a dozen books on the presidency, asserts that Kennedy was a reformer, but a cautious one. While Kennedy understood the moral imperative of supporting such civil rights efforts as the Freedom Rides, he waited for the most politically productive opportunities to voice his eloquent support for civil rights.

The White House, he asserted, "must be the center of moral leadership." But on some of the pressing moral issues of the day, Kennedy was a reluctant reformer. He avoided civil rights until it became politically unacceptable to do so. Was this wisdom or cowardice? As FDR knew, it was dangerous to get too far out in front of public opinion. Kennedy waited until the civil rights issue gained prominence, then became its champion.

As Kennedy took office, the civil rights movement was picking up steam. Several violent confrontations between demonstrators and police officials made headline news. In Mississippi and Alabama, reactionary governors tried to prevent black students from enrolling in state universities.

nedy himself seems largely to have remained detached from executive action, at least in the beginning.

He did personally intervene in some cases. On Inauguration Day, Kennedy himself noticed that the honor guards in the parade were all white and moved to ensure that the various military branches were desegregating, both in the honor guard setting and in their admissions to the service academies. Another exception was JFK's letter to General U.S. Grant III on the eve of the one hundredth anniversary of the beginning of the Civil War at Fort Sumter, South Carolina. Grant chaired the National Civil War Commission and had scheduled the centennial event at a segregated hotel which would not house Negro delegates. Kennedy

---

Riots followed. "Freedom riders" flocked into the South, hoping to work for racial equality. At first Kennedy was a "reluctant revolutionary," but as events built to the boiling point, the president intervened. Blacks desperately needed the moral force of the presidency to help their cause. Kennedy obliged. Speaking over national television from the Oval Office, Kennedy said the nation faced a "moral crisis as a country and a people." This cannot be the land of the free "except for the Negroes. . . . The heart of the question is whether all Americans are to be afforded equal rights and equal opportunities, whether we are going to treat our fellow Americans as we want to be treated." Then, in an especially moving passage, he said, "We cannot say to 10 percent of the population that you can't have that right; that your children can't have the chance to develop whatever talents they have; that the only way that they are going to get their rights is to go into the streets and demonstrate. I think we owe them and we owe ourselves a better country than that."

Michael A. Genovese, *The Power of the American Presidency: 1789–2000*. New York: Oxford University Press, 2001, p. 151.

wrote to Grant urging him "to take action which would assure that the arrangements . . . meet the standards set for us by the Constitution and by our moral conscience.". . .

Symbolic and Legal Action

In the Justice Department, there were symbolic acts and legal actions. Robert Kennedy resigned from the Metropolitan Club because of its racial policies, prompting journalist Carl Rowan to write to RFK that his action marked a "marvelous move for a nation that for so long has desperately needed this kind of moral leadership at your level." And Robert Kennedy, concerned about the scarcity of black attorneys at Justice, wrote a letter to deans of many law schools asking them to identify "qualified Negro attorneys of your acquaintance who might be interested in coming to the Department" so that he might "break down the barrier" of race.

In legal action, Burke Marshall took charge of civil rights policy in the Justice Department. His year-end reports show extensive activity. In voting rights, the Kennedy administration prosecuted six voting discrimination suits held over from the Eisenhower years and filed twelve more in its first year. The administration also attempted to lessen employment discrimination, especially in the federal government. In school desegregation, Marshall argued that Justice moved "with vigor to protect the integrity of the court orders, to preserve the due administration of justice and to encourage and assist local officials and community leaders who are effective in promoting peaceful desegregation of the schools."

Meanwhile, as the Kennedy administration pursued low-profile tactics, civil rights advocates began to be critical of the administration's pace. The National Committee against Discrimination in Housing noted in September of 1961 that it had been "thirteen months since he promised that the new Democratic administration would act and eight months since he took office," but still there was no executive order concerning housing. Wofford began to be frustrated that Kennedy would not meet with black leaders such as the leaders of the Student Nonviolent Coordinating Committee (SNCC), arguing that "it would be better for the President to see them for ten or fifteen minutes than to wait until they launch fasts in jail or encampments outside the White House asking to see him."

Freedom Rides

The first important civil rights activity of Kennedy's presidency came in the form of the freedom rides in May of 1961. On April 26, 1961, James Farmer, the leader of the freedom ride movement, wrote to JFK that the rides were an expression "of our duty to affirm our principles by asserting our rights. With the survival of democracy at stake, there is an imperative, immediate need for acts of self-determination." Although Kennedy tried to postpone the rides so they would not interfere with his upcoming meeting with French President Charles de Gaulle and Soviet leader Nikita Khrushchev, the administration supported the riders, asserting for the nation the rights of citizens to travel on integrated transportation. Kennedy called out the National Guard, obtained a federal court order enjoining segregationists from interfering with interstate bus travel, and issued a statement calling for the restoration of order in Alabama. When pushed, the Kennedys were willing to bring the full power of the national government to bear in these affairs.

But the rhetoric of the president and the attorney general did not embrace the movement. Kennedy expressed the feeling that "there's no question of the legal rights of the freedom travelers—Freedom riders, to move in interstate commerce," indicating that he would use federal power to insure that right if necessary. Rather than making the moral argument about human rights, he said "the basic question

is not the Freedom Riders. The basic question is that anyone who moves in interstate commerce should be able to
do so freely." Instead of embracing the movement. Kennedy saw the freedom rides as a simple question of legality. . . .

Confrontation and Crisis

In 1963, perhaps the most dramatic of civil rights events
came with violent confrontations between civil rights activists, led by Dr. Martin Luther King, Jr. and segregationists, led by police head "Bull" Connor, in Birmingham, Alabama. In early May, civil rights marchers were arrested and
others were beaten. The administration sympathized with
the movement and acted strongly to help keep the situation
from spinning out of control. Again, however, the president
seemed to define the incidents in Birmingham to limit the
national government commitment to keeping the peace.
While there was negotiation between Robert Kennedy and
Dr. King about the timing of the marches, and while the
Justice Department sent Burke Marshall to Birmingham to
try to mediate between civil rights marchers and white
leaders, the federal government's intervention did not go
any further. President Kennedy stated that "There isn't any
federal statute that was involved in the last few days in Birmingham, Alabama." Again, the president apparently
wished to limit his role as a leader in the move for civil
rights, using the issue of federalism as a convenient crutch.

Birmingham, however, was seen by Martin Luther King
and others as a critical changing point. In a sense, they felt
that Kennedy was "born again" to the movement. That
seemingly new commitment coincided with the major civil
rights event of the summer of 1963—the March on Washington. And its confirmation came in a switch in tactics by
the Kennedy administration—moving from an executive
strategy to a legislative one with the introduction in 1963 of
an Omnibus Civil Rights Bill. As events unfolded, Kennedy's rhetorical style also changed. In a June 11 speech,

rather than defining the struggle in legal terms, Kennedy said "We are confronted primarily with a moral issue. It is as old as the Scriptures and as clear as the American Constitution. . . ." And his message to Congress pushing the passage of his Civil Rights Bill contained some of the most emotional appeals of his presidency:

> I ask you to look into your hearts—not in search of charity, for the Negro neither needs nor wants condescension—but for one plain, proud, and priceless quality that unites us as Americans: a sense of justice. In this year of the Emancipation Centennial, justice requires us to insure the blessings of liberty for all Americans and their posterity—not merely for reasons of economic efficiency, world diplomacy and domestic tranquility—but, above all, because it is right."

Choices

Yet these changes did not make Kennedy a complete convert to the cause. He still wanted to exercise control over the flow of the issue. In a meeting with civil rights leaders before the March on Washington, Kennedy expressed the hope that the March could be called off. While movement leaders saw the March as a way to mobilize support for the civil rights bill, Kennedy feared that the March might cause a "white backlash" that would jeopardize its passage. Again, Kennedy's pragmatic approach reveals a lack of empathy for the depth of feeling among the black leadership or that civil rights leaders wished to be involved in legislative strategy. It would have been ironic had the leaders of the civil rights movement left such a dramatic legislative battle and policy leadership of the issue to an almost entirely white legislature and executive. When the March occurred, it was with the assistance of the administration and resulted in Martin Luther King's famous "I have a dream" speech. . . .

With regard to the civil rights measure itself, how is

Kennedy to be judged? The 1963 Civil Rights bill was, as might be expected, criticized from both the left and the right. Critics of the left wanted to toughen the bill, while Kennedy wished to pursue a more moderate bill because he thought such a measure would be more easily passed. While the bill was not passed in Kennedy's lifetime, he had finally warmed to the legislative battle. When the bill was at last proposed. Kennedy pursued it with vengeance. . . .

Assessing Kennedy's Legacy

In assessing Kennedy, both in terms of his personal and presidential commitment to civil rights, several generalizations can be made. First, Kennedy eventually had a strong policy commitment to civil rights. He made civil rights pledges during the 1960 campaign and he never seriously wavered when confronted with civil rights conflict. His understanding of the racial politics of the South might have been lacking, but in terms of his own policy preference, Kennedy advocated civil rights reform.

It is equally clear that at least for the first two years of his presidency, civil rights was not an issue of primary importance to Kennedy. While his principal civil rights policy adviser, Harris Wofford, recommended that Kennedy pursue an executive strategy early in his administration, Kennedy was seemingly happy to leave the issue to routine administration rather than presidential leadership. During this period the president was involved in civil rights, but his involvement was apparently always a reaction to events forced by the Civil Rights Movement rather than one precipitated by any presidential initiative. And when he made public statements, they involved straightforward pronouncements concerning keeping the peace and following the law rather than broad-sweeping moral pronouncements about the inherent moral issues involved. While Kennedy was interested in exercising the full amount of presidential power in the arena of foreign policy, using his charismatic personality to its fullest, he always seemed a little more restrained in pursuit of civil rights. [Presidential scholar Richard] Neustadt attributes his reserved approach to civil rights to the fact that "he had a distaste for preaching, really for the preachiness of politics, backed by genuine mistrust of mass emotion as a tool in politics." In contrast, recalling the Kennedy era, the late Supreme Court Justice Thurgood Marshall attributed Kennedy's style to a relative reluctance to carry the torch of civil rights policy. He said that "at any time that it would be necessary for the federal arm of the government to move, specifically the executive arm, that I was convinced that the President was determined to use the full force of his office, whenever it became necessary. But *not* until it became necessary."

Once Kennedy decided on a legislative strategy, he pursued that initiative vigorously. By his third year in office, whether through being forced into a leadership position by southern segregationist leaders or by having seen the moral nature of the civil rights policy arena, Kennedy had warmed to the issue. He appeared willing to talk of the issue in moral terms and he also became personally involved in the legislative battle. . . .

On balance, the Kennedy record seems quite consistent with the revisionist interpretation. He deserves credit for his exercise of leadership in civil rights, but his leadership was largely of a reactive sort, with events constantly being forced upon him by civil rights activists. Only when the legislative game came into play during the summer of 1963 did Kennedy's role approximate that of a protagonist. Kennedy pushed civil rights further than any president previously had, but barring some unforeseen revelations about his personal convictions on civil rights, we may never know the depth or intensity of his own views.

Kennedy's Enforcement of Desegregation at the University of Mississippi Demonstrated His Commitment to Civil Rights

Theodore C. Sorensen

"Ole Miss" was an all-white university until a black student named James Meredith attempted to enroll. This attempt at desegregation was met with hostility and political opposition in Mississippi. Meredith's actions touched off nothing short of a political firestorm—where the governor, police, and military would ultimately become involved in the case. Kennedy and his brother Robert (his attorney general) managed to resolve the standoff with segregationist leaders and overcome the limited legal options of the federal government to intervene in state affairs, while desegregating the state university. The case demonstrates the sensitivity and complexity of civil rights policy in the Deep South facing Kennedy. The author, Theodore C. Sorensen, served as special counsel to President Kennedy.

Theodore C. Sorensen, *Kennedy*. New York: Harper & Row, 1965. Copyright © 1965 by Theodore C. Sorensen. All rights reserved. Reproduced by permission of Harper-Collins Publishers.

THE ISSUE ORIGINALLY PITTED NEGRO APPLICANT JAMES Meredith against the all-white University of Mississippi. It eventually and unavoidably pitted the state of Mississippi against the United States. It was termed at the time the most serious clash of state versus Federal authority since the end of the Civil War; and its favorable resolution upheld not only the principle of equal rights and the sanctity of law but also the paramount powers of the Presidency.

Well over a year earlier, Meredith had attempted to enroll in the tax-supported public university located at Oxford in his native state. A long series of court rulings, all the way up to the Supreme Court, ordered his admission and an end to official resistance. When open and avowed defiance continued in a manner unprecedented for a century, the United States Court of Appeals for the Fifth Circuit—consisting of eight Southern jurists—found Mississippi's Governor Ross Barnett and Lieutenant Governor Paul Johnson guilty of contempt for blocking Meredith's admission. The judges, their patience exhausted, then directed the Federal Government to enforce the court's order and to put down what bordered on rebellion.

Enter Kennedy

The President and Attorney General accepted this responsibility and moved steadily but cautiously to meet it. They hoped to avoid either force or violence in the most thoroughly segregated, bitterly prejudiced state in the Federal Union. They hoped to avoid making a martyr out of Governor Barnett, who was rumored to be planning a Senate race against the more thoughtful and soft-spoken John Stennis. They hoped to persuade Mississippi officials—and ultimately did persuade the university officials—to comply peacefully and responsibly with the law. They hoped, finally, to prove that many steps lay between inaction and the use of Federal troops—including a few, many or a full squadron of U.S. marshals (including deputies, border patrolmen and Federal prison guards) especially trained for such situations.

In late September of 1962 matters came rapidly to a head. Nearly every day of the last ten days of the month a new effort was made—in court, at the university, at the State College Board, at the Governor's office or with the Governor privately by telephone. Each day the number of marshals accompanying Meredith grew larger. Each conversation with Barnett grew sharper. Bob Kennedy and his brilliant Assistant Attorney General Burke Marshall led the fight, thus re-emphasizing that it was not John F. Kennedy whom Barnett defied but the majesty of the United States Government.

Finally, on Sunday, September 30, Barnett recognized the inevitable. The President had issued a proclamation and Executive Order preliminary to federalizing the Mississippi National Guard and deploying other troops. He had announced a nationwide TV address for Sunday night. In a series of secret telephone conversations with the Attorney General and the President, Barnett suggested that he be permitted to stand courageously in the door of the school and yield only when a marshal's gun was pointed at him. But that little drama would have risked violence from menacing groups of students, sheriffs, state police and hangers-on who gathered for each such confrontation. Still trying to save face, the Governor then proposed that Meredith be spirited quickly and quietly onto the campus that very day, Sunday, before the President's speech. Inasmuch as it had been assumed that the speech would announce Federal action for Monday, the Oxford campus would be deserted for the weekend, the Governor could pretend ignorance and he then would protest vehemently from his office at Jackson. A large force of state police would assure the safety of Meredith, Barnett promised, with no need for National Guardsmen or other forces. The Kennedys agreed to the plan as a means of avoiding Barnett's arrest and a troop deployment but, unwilling to rely wholly on Barnett's word, they kept troops on a stand-by basis in Memphis and equipped Meredith's guard of deputy marshals with steel helmets and tear gas. . . .

The Moment of Truth

I arrived to find the President . . . pacing the floor of the Cabinet Room, where a direct phone link to Oxford was being maintained. His speech had been set for 7:30 P.M. Sunday night, and by the time that hour arrived Meredith, escorted by state police and university officials, had been driven safely to a men's dormitory on the campus. But the President was still skeptical of Barnett's pledge. "We can't take a chance with Meredith's life," he said to his brother, "or let that——make the Federal Government look foolish." He postponed his talk until 10 P.M. The possibility of domestic violence made him more anxious than usual. He carefully rewrote his speech to make it clear that the government was merely carrying out the orders of the court in a case it had not brought and was not forcing anything down the throats of Mississippians on its own initiative.

Meanwhile a squad of U.S. deputy marshals—which in the end reached 550—took up guard positions near the university administration building, deliberately staying away from Meredith's unpublicized quarters. It was not an army. All were civilians, most were from the South, and many worked in Immigration or other Justice Department offices unaccustomed to armed combat. But they were well disciplined under the leadership of Chief Marshal James Mc-Shane and Deputy Attorney General Nicholas Katzenbach. Throughout the night these men and other Justice officials on the scene maintained direct telephone contact with the "Command Headquarters" set up in the Cabinet Room, because of the camera crews working in the President's office.

By 10 P.M., when the President went on the air, Barnett had already issued his statement, claiming that Meredith had been sneaked in "by helicopter" without his knowledge. His aides informed the White House that no further forces would be required. But the two hundred state police he provided had suddenly vanished without notice at the first sign of tension, returning only after a bitter protest to the Governor's office from the Attorney General. Now an ugly mob was gathering around the band of marshals as the President began to speak.

The speech, its first rough draft prepared the night before in the hospital but its final text completed by the President only shortly before air time, began with a quiet statement of fact and hope:

> The orders of the court in the case of *Meredith versus Fair* are beginning to be carried out. . . . This has been accomplished thus far without the use of National Guard or other troops.

The President then gave a brief but eloquent summation on "the integrity of American law":

> Our nation is founded on the principle that observance of the law is the eternal safeguard of liberty. . . . Even among law-abiding men, few laws are universally loved, but they are uniformly respected and not resisted. Americans are free to disagree with the law, but not to disobey it. . . . My obligation . . . is to implement the orders of the court with whatever means are necessary, and with as little force and civil disorder as the circumstances permit.

An Appeal to Reason

Reviewing the circumstances of the case, he emphasized the Southern backgrounds of the Federal judges, commended other Southern universities that had admitted Negroes and pointed out that only Mississippi's failure to do likewise had brought the Federal Government into the picture. Reminding his Mississippi listeners of that state's history of patriotic courage, he concluded with an appeal to the students of the university, the people who were most concerned.

> You have a great tradition to uphold, a tradition of honor and courage. . . . Let us preserve both the law and the peace, and then, healing those wounds that are within, we can turn to the greater crises that are without, and stand united as one people in our pledge to man's freedom.

The great majority of students, however, did not hear or heed the President's appeal. Nor did the great majority of the more than 2,500 roughnecks who began attacking newsmen and marshals—even as the President was speaking—have any connection with the university. Roughnecks and racists from all over Mississippi and the South had been gathering in Oxford, carrying clubs, rocks, pipes, bricks, bottles, bats, firebombs—and guns. The marshals responded with tear gas but kept their pistols in their holsters. The Attorney General's continuing efforts to enlist the effective help of university officials—including the popular and successful football coach—were in vain. The arrival of the local Mississippi National Guard unit only enraged the Guard's fellow Mississippians further. As rioting raged through the night, a newsman and a townsman were shot dead, two hundred marshals and Guardsmen were injured, vehicles and buildings were burned, campus benches were smashed to provide jagged concrete projectiles, a stolen fire engine and bulldozer tried to batter their way into the administration building and frenzied attackers roamed the campus. But the Governor had failed to reassign the state police in force; and the President, who had previously thought it best to deal with Barnett chiefly through the Attorney General, angrily took the phone and demanded of the Governor that he send his police back. He interrupted each of Barnett's drawled excuses and explanations. "Listen, Governor, somebody's been shot down there already and it's going to get worse. Most of it's happened since those police left and I want them back. Goodbye." He slammed down the phone.

Orders and Disorder

Barnett had whined, grumbled and equivocated, afraid that his compatriots knew he had "sold out," begging that Meredith be withdrawn, but finally agreeing to send the two hundred state troopers back. More crucial time passed, however, before fifty showed up to stay. In a new statement, which reversed his earlier statement of merely indignant submission, the Governor proclaimed that Mississippi would "never surrender." Perhaps he reasoned that mob action could achieve his aims without placing him directly in contempt of court.

In His Own Way, Kennedy Understood Discrimination

James David Barber, well known for his work on presidential personalities, examines the psychological basis for Kennedy's commitment to civil rights.

The Kennedy way of looking at the world, in its broad outlines, grew from the same family soil. There was first the fact of being Irish in a town with an Irish mayor but a community and, to a large degree, a business world dominated by the Boston Protestants. Irish-ism to old Joe Kennedy meant fierce resentment at discrimination, carried in his memory from tales of his immigrant grandfather and his saloonkeeper father who struggled to give his son a better chance. Joe Sr. left Boston for New York and Hollywood to make money—but also to get away from the firm prejudices Massachusetts kept demonstrating to him. He bought a summer

The marshals—bloodied, unfed and exhausted—obeyed orders to use only the minimum tear gas necessary to protect lives and to refrain from returning fire. But their telephoned reports to the President and Attorney General expressed concern about snipers in the dark and uncertainty as to how much longer they could hold out even with National Guard help. The President, terribly disheartened by news of increasing violence, especially against the Federal marshals, and concerned lest the mob run rampant, find James Meredith and lynch him, ordered into action the troops standing by in Memphis. Their response was agonizingly slow. Each time he called the Pentagon the troops were "on their way." Each new call from Oxford asked desperately where they were. His temper rising, the President insisted on talking directly to the Army commander on the scene. An elaborate Army communication system failed to func-

place in Cohasset, a favorite watering place for Old Boston families, but was blackballed when he tried to join the country club. "It was petty and cruel," a friend said. "The women in Cohasset looked down on the daughter of 'Honey Fitz'; and who was Joe Kennedy but the son of Pat, the barkeeper?" When Jack was at Harvard, Rose once asked an uppercrust friend of his, "Tell me, when are the nice people of Boston going to accept us?" Everywhere Joe went—including Harvard—he seemed to run into prejudice against the Irish. "I was born here. My children were born here. What the hell do I have to do to be an American?" he demanded to know. In his own life he gave the answer: win. By the time his children grew up, prejudice against them for their heritage was on the wane, but Jack ran hard up against it in 1960 when he reached for the top.

James David Barber, *The Presidential Character: Predicting Performance in the White House*. Englewood Cliffs, NJ: Prentice-Hall, 1992, p. 349.

tion, and the President received his reports from Katzenbach dropping dimes into a pay phone in a campus booth.

We were all tired and hungry now, with an almost helpless feeling about getting the troops there in time to relieve the hard-pressed defenders. The President looked drawn and bleak. He refused to accept our suggestion that he had done everything he could. Through the long night of waiting and telephoning, he cursed himself for ever believing Barnett and for not ordering the troops in sooner. . . .

The End and the Beginning

Once the flow of troops began, it gushed forth in what were soon needless numbers of up to twenty thousand. The mob was dispersed; the town was quieted; some two hundred troublemakers were arrested; and Barnett issued still another statement, this one opposing violence. Early the next morning Meredith, accompanied by a group of marshals (at least one of whom would be guarding him constantly thereafter) but not, at the President's insistence, by Army troops, officially registered and began, to the jeers and catcalls of his fellow students, his own ordeal of perseverance.

Governor Barnett, embarrassed by the revelation that he had double-crossed his own segregationist supporters by conniving in Meredith's admission on Sunday, sought to blame "trigger-happy" marshals for starting the trouble, a charge echoed not only by some Senators but by some university officials who knew better. The Governor ignored the injuries suffered by eight marshals before the tear gas was fired in self-protection, the thirty-five marshals shot and the more than 150 others requiring medical treatment. He claimed that the state police gas masks were not suitable for tear gas. And he complained, just as the rest of the world marveled, that the Federal Government had arrayed thousands of troops and spent several hundred thousands of dollars to obtain the admission of one otherwise obscure citizen to the university.

But "this country cannot survive . . . and this government would unravel very fast," said the President, "if . . . the Executive Branch does not carry out the decisions of the court . . . [or] had failed . . . to protect Mr. Meredith. . . . That would have been far more expensive." The cost of the Meredith incident, he reasoned, could be spread over all the other incidents avoided in the peaceful admissions that would follow. "I recognize that it has caused a lot of bitterness against me," he added. "[But] I don't really know what other role they would expect the President of the United States to play. They expect me to carry out my oath under the Constitution, and that is what we are going to do."

He sought to heal "those wounds that are within." He resisted a Civil Rights Commission recommendation that he shut off all Federal funds to Mississippi, regardless of whether they aided whites or Negroes, integrated or segregated activities, believing that no President should possess the power to punish an entire state. He urged through Burke Marshall that an indignant Court of Appeals punish Barnett's contempt by fine instead of by the martyrdom of arrest and imprisonment. He urged other states to realize that all court orders would be carried out and that resistance served no purpose other than their own economic harm. He was pleased that quiet preparations with South Carolina leaders, as well as the force of example in Mississippi, helped facilitate the peaceful admission to Clemson University of its first Negro student. But he knew that the Mississippi battle was not an end but a beginning—that his relations with the South would never be the same— and that still harsher crises and choices lay ahead in 1963.

PRESIDENTS
and their
DECISIONS

CHAPTER

4

THE SPACE RACE

Science, Politics, and the Origins of the Space Race

Charles Lam Markmann and Mark Sherwin

The United States was embarrassed by the Soviet Union's successful launch of *Sputnik* in 1957. This and successive efforts in space by the Soviets persuaded Kennedy that the United States was losing the space race and, more important, the scientific race. In leading the American space program, Kennedy showed himself to be a visionary. But he also had to balance concerns about high costs, the need to use private contractors, and promoting scientific research for such purposes as national security, ocean resource management, and food production. All of these factors shaped his decisions on space. Charles Lam Markmann and Mark Sherwin are authors who have written extensively on Kennedy.

I N APRIL A PHOTOGRAPH THAT APPEARED IN ALMOST ALL newspapers throughout the world showed the President watching television. He was standing in the office of his secretary, Mrs. Evelyn Lincoln, hands in his pockets. At his left was Mrs. Kennedy, leaning on a desk. Behind him stood his brother, Robert, McGeorge Bundy, Vice President Johnson, Arthur Schlesinger and Admiral Burke. Their eyes were fixed on the screen, which was showing them a Redstone

Charles Lam Markmann and Mark Sherwin, *John F. Kennedy: A Sense of Purpose*. New York: St. Martin's Press, 1961.

rocket about to carry Alan B. Shepard Jr., a Navy commander, into space. It was America's biggest publicity gamble.

At this stage in the Kennedy Administration, American
prestige and morale were at their lowest. The Russians had
already sent a man into orbit; the Cuban tragedy was still
fresh in the minds of the people, as were the retreats in
strategic Southeast Asia. There had been strong voices that
had urged Kennedy to postpone the shot indefinitely, fear-
ing that failure would plunge America's position even
lower, if that were possible. There were the timid who had
criticized the tremendous publicity buildup the space shot
had been given. A week before, a similar shot, unmanned,
had been destroyed shortly after blast-off, but, when the
Cape Canaveral command had looked to Kennedy, he
replied: "You may proceed when ready."

For 15 anxious minutes Kennedy and the nation
watched as the space capsule named *Freedom 7* carried the
160-pound Shepard in an arc that reached an altitude of
115 miles and set him down 302 miles away in the sea off
the Bahama Islands. The relieved nation cheered and the
world applauded.

The triumph for the United States was not tarnished by
the technical difference between Shepard's feat and the
flight of Yuri Gagarin. Shepard had attained a top speed of
only 4,500 miles an hour and had traveled a short distance
in comparison with the Russian's total orbit of the earth at
a speed of 18,000 miles an hour and an altitude of more
than 188 miles. Gagarin was only a passenger in his capsule, while Shepard was able to control some of the actions
of his vehicle. Both saw the earth and described it. Both
suffered no ill effects from their voyages. Both were enthusiastic. Both were sportsmen. Gagarin said: "There's
enough space in the cosmos for all. American cosmonauts
will have to catch up with us. We shall welcome their success, but will try to keep in front." Shepard echoed these
sentiments. . . .

Origins of the Space Race

Immediately after World War II, when Germany had proved the value of the rocket as a weapon, the Soviet Government assigned a high priority to missile development and proceeded with an admirable single-mindedness to pursue and develop all forms of boosters from liquid and solid fuels to atomic power. There was no interference from dissidents because there were no dissidents.

It was different, however, in the United States. Ironically, the first liquid-fueled rocket was launched in 1926 in America by Robert H. Goddard, But, like Russia, the United States was impressed by the German rockets and proceeded in 1945 to initiate a program with the aid of German rocket experts who had been "induced" to come to America. Under the leadership of Wernher von Braun, 110 scientists, considered the cream of German rocketry, began to work on plans that were regarded with casual indifference by a military traditionally suspicious of innovations and "gadgets." Between 1945 and 1957 the American space projects suffered from pessimism and penny-pinching founded on pernicious complacency.

Vannevar Bush, director of the wartime Office of Scientific Research and Development, looked upon the idea of a 3,000-mile military missile as unrealistic. "I don't think anybody in the world knows how to do such a thing," he said. "I feel confident that it will not be done for a long time." In those days, the atomic bomb weighed 10,000 pounds, which was an inconceivable load for a rocket to carry. Big bombers such as the B-29 were regarded as the best system for delivering the atomic bomb. The attitude of the military and civilian experts began to change by 1951, when the Korean war was in progress and the cold war had brought demands for experimentation in advanced weapons. The Air Force began work on the Atlas missile, its booster scaled to the needs of carrying a nuclear warhead. . . .

The United States was forced into action in 1957 when

Sputniks I and *II* went up. By this time the American program was woefully behind Soviet development. The National Aeronautics and Space Agency was set up a year later with orders to proceed at headlong speed "and never mind the cost," but officials sadly observed that money was not a complete substitute for time.

Sputnik and Redstone

After Gagarin's flight Kennedy appeared at a press conference and for the first time gave the impression of being visibly shaken by a Russian victory. His answers were slow and plodding and he repeated several times that the Russians had bigger boosters and we would try to catch up. No one doubted that the United States would catch up, but when was another problem. "The news," the President said, "will be worse before it gets better. It will be some time before we catch up . . . and I'm sure they [the Russians] are making a concentrated effort to stay ahead."

Shepard's success in his Redstone heartened those working on the space program. A big booster rocket, the F-1 Nova, was tested successfully on the ground and showed great promise. But the main hopes were centered on the *Saturn*, with a thrust of 1.5 million pounds, which was expected to be ready by 1964 and help the United States catch up with the Russians in 1965. In that year, the United States planned to launch Project Apollo, a three-man orbiting space ship that would ride atop the giant *Saturn*. Robert C. Seamans, associate director of NASA, said the United States might be able to put a man on the moon by 1967. "It is a date that could be considered from a planning standpoint," he told Congress. The cost was placed at $5 billion.

Why Space?

There were, of course, many earth-bound thinkers who saw no sense or reason in the mad race for space. In a mass Washington interview, Commander Shepard neatly turned aside a question on how his flight was going to benefit the hungry and the needy of the world. But this was the historic argument against all scientific experimentation. Sociologists, scientists and historians had too many precedents to cite in rebuttal to make the argument even interesting. It was true that for the moment experiments in space travel were tied to military urgencies and ideological rivalries, but most people seemed to understand that man was following a cosmic destiny that had begun in the cave and

The Symbolism of *Sputnik*

David Burner, the author of John F. Kennedy: A New Generation, *suggests that the launching of the Soviet satellite* Sputnik *in 1957 shocked the nation into action.*

The launching of *Sputnik*, which triggered much of the national anxiety of the late 1950s, quickened a national self-examination. The Russian superiority suggested that our schools were inadequate to train scientists and technicians to be equally proficient, inadequate especially to school young Americans in diligence and an appetite for achievement. Previously, conformity had been a topic among the more widely read social critics. Now it seemed that conformity within the middle classes might be an explanation of why American youth lacked the will and resilience to match the Soviet success. The nation appeared to be failing in the very virtues that it most prized as its foundation and its proper object. And it was the liberal rather than the conservative temper that was the readier to concern itself with the kinds of excellence that were at issue.

David Burner, *John F. Kennedy and a New Generation*. Glenview, IL: Scott, Foresman/Little, Brown, 1988, pp. 42–43.

had moved inexorably forward.

Time Magazine speculated that, "even if the deadly Russian-American rivalry that now supports most space research should die out, men will surely continue their struggle to escape from their own globe. For, in the end, space victories do not belong to any particular nation. They are achievements of the science and technology of the human species, the result of man's urge to explore the unknown."

There was really no need to explain or apologize because there was sufficient evidence in the sky that some practical application of the space race had been achieved. The Russians and the Americans had sent up satellites covering various scientific requirements. In addition to sun probes, moon probes, a shot at Venus, instruments were orbiting the earth sending back weather data, information on cosmic rays and radiation zones, and other knowledge to be used in the pure as well as the applied sciences. Tracking stations throughout the world were keeping in touch, harvesting information from space in a manner that had become mostly routine and ordinary. . . .

Science for the Future

Of all the complications, the problem that confronted the President was who would get the first contract. The first and most practical solution was to give it to a consortium of all the bidders. NASA, still working for the Government alone, planned to launch the first of a series of new communication satellites within a year. The Pentagon was also working on Project Advent for armed-services communications. The private companies were eagerly following the progress of these two plans, hoping somehow to get into the space program with Government blessing and their own funds. In this commercial area there was no reason to believe that the Russians were ahead of the United States, which had long experience in the understanding of how to work for profit.

While almost everyone was looking up into space, the President, considering population growth and food problems, cast a look at the ocean and made it part of his "science for the future" program.

As a long-range investment in the future of all mankind, Kennedy asked Congress to consider the richness of "the seas around us." He presented an impressive statistical portrait—the Pacific, the Atlantic, the Indian and the Arctic Oceans accounting for an expanse of 130 million square miles; the Mediterranean, the Bering, the Malay, the Black, the Red and 13 other seas covering 10 million more square miles, and the depth of all making 330 million cubic miles. In a letter to Johnson, in his capacity as President of the Senate, Kennedy said: "We are just at the threshold of our knowledge of the oceans. This is more than a matter of curiosity. Our very survival may hinge upon it." He then urged Congress to appropriate $97.5 million for various ventures in oceanography designed to develop future sources of food and minerals. This basic research, he pointed out, would include new studies in weather forecasting and possible weather control. It would also be of immediate benefit to the Navy in its undersea operations.

Kennedy showed that at present about one percent of mankind's food came from the ocean and more would be needed soon. "The seas offer a wealth of nutritional resources," he wrote Johnson. "They already are principal sources of protein. They can provide many times the current food supply if we but learn how to garner and husband this self-renewing larder. To meet the vast needs of an expanding population, the bounty of the sea must be made more available. Within two decades our nation will require over 1 million more tons (a year) of seafood than we can now harvest."

New Frontiers

The program was received with elation by oceanographers generally and in particular by Dr. Harris B. Stewart Jr., chief oceanographer of the Coast and Geodetic Survey. "Nothing like it has ever come from the White House," Dr. Stewart said. "Most of our resources on land are gradually running out. People are starving in the world, and the seas are full of food. Over the course of geological time the earth has been eroding into the sea, so the sea is now the great sink-hole of the mineral resources drained from the land, including such vital industrial necessities as salt, potassium, manganese, nickel and cobalt. Off the West Coast we photographed whole areas of the bottom of the sea littered with manganese nodules the size of an orange or grapefruit. These nodules are rich in nickel and cobalt as well. Here is untapped wealth. Through basic research we may be able to learn the mechanism by which these nodules are made."

Dr. Stewart emphasized the point made by the President that "this is not a one-year program or even a ten-year program. It is the first step in a continuing effort to acquire and apply the information about a part of our world that will ultimately determine conditions of life in the rest of the world." As a beginning, the President proposed that the money would be spent in the next fiscal year on ten new oceanographic vessels, laboratories, wharfside facilities and basic research.

If the President needed encouragement as he contemplated his future travails in the space race, in the advances of all the sciences and in striving for a richer and better life for his nation, he received it from a most unexpected quarter. It came from Nikita Khrushchev in the moment of triumph when Russia had sent the first man into orbit around the earth. He looked with wistful envy toward America when he told all the Russians: "The space flight must not distract the attention of the Soviet people from other targets, and these include catching up with the United States in the standard of living."

Kennedy Acted Boldly in Winning the Space Race

Theodore C. Sorensen

Theodore C. Sorensen, who served as special counsel to President Kennedy, maintains that Kennedy believed the space gap between the Soviet Union and the United States was a potentially dangerous threat to national security. Acting on this belief, Sorensen suggests Kennedy saw the problem more clearly than his advisers. In spite of opposition in Congress and in the face of possible further scientific and political embarrassment, Kennedy acted boldly and admirably in leading America to success in the race for space.

I N HIS 1961 ADDRESS TO THE UNITED NATIONS, THE PRESIdent called for peaceful cooperation in a new domain—outer space. "The cold reaches of the universe," he said, "must not become the new arena of an even colder war." In both his Inaugural and first State of the Union addresses that year, he had called for East-West cooperation "to invoke the wonders of science instead of its terrors. Together let us explore the stars."

But the Soviets had brusquely rejected the suggestion. They had little incentive to cooperate with an American space program which lagged far behind their own—not in

Theodore C. Sorensen, *Kennedy*. New York: Harper & Row, 1965. Copyright © 1965 by Theodore C. Sorensen. All rights reserved. Reproduced by permission of HarperCollins Publishers.

the number and variety of scientific studies but in the all-important capacity to lift large payloads into orbit. With their more powerful rocket boosters—developed originally to launch more massive nuclear warheads before they learned the technique of the small hydrogen bomb—the Soviets in 1957 were the first to launch a space satellite, then the first to put living animals into orbit. The Eisenhower administration, despite prodding from Majority Leader Johnson, started its own program slowly and tardily, with much scoffing and skepticism from Republican officials about the meaning of the Russian effort. President Truman had also cut back the infant American space program started after the war with the help of German scientists.

The Space Gap

John Kennedy had borne down hard on this space gap in the 1960 campaign. To him it symbolized the nation's lack of initiative, ingenuity and vitality under Republican rule. He was convinced that Americans did not yet fully grasp the world-wide political and psychological impact of the space race. With East and West competing to convince the new and undecided nations which way to turn, which wave was the future, the dramatic Soviet achievements, he feared, were helping to build a dangerous impression of unchallenged world leadership generally and scientific pre-eminence particularly. American scientists could repeat over and over that the more solid contributions of our own space research were a truer measure of national strength, but neither America nor the world paid much attention.

After the election, a top-notch transition task force under Jerome Wiesner had warned Kennedy that the United States could not win the race to put a man in space. Others expressed concern that a Soviet space monopoly would bring new military dangers and disadvantages to the West. Our own rocket thrust was adequate for all known military purposes, but no one could be certain of its future uses. Other nations, moreover, assumed that a Soviet space lead meant a missile lead as well; and whether this assumption was true or false, it affected their attitudes in the cold war.

Before his first hundred days in the White House were out, Kennedy's concern was dramatically proven correct. Moscow announced on April 12 that Cosmonaut Yuri Gagarin had completed an orbital flight around the earth in less than two hours. As the Soviet Union capitalized on its historic feat in all corners of the globe, Kennedy congratulated Khrushchev and Gagarin—and set to work.

The U.S. Response

He had already sharply increased the budget request for development of the large Saturn rocket booster; and he had already revitalized the National Space Council, with the Vice President as Chairman, to expedite progress with less military-civilian quibbling. But that was not enough. Nor was he reassured on the day after the Gagarin announcement when National Aeronautics and Space Administrator James Webb brought in a desk model of the U.S.-designed capsule soon to carry an American astronaut into space. Eyeing the Rube Goldberg–like contraption on his desk, Kennedy speculated that Webb might have bought it in a toy store on his way to work that morning.

To gain some immediate answers, he asked me to review with Wiesner that same day—in preparation for an interview he had granted for that evening—the outlook in NASA and the Budget Bureau on next steps in the space race. NASA reported that the dramatic big-booster steps still to come might include, in possible order of development, longer one-man orbits, two men in a spacecraft, an orbiting space laboratory, a fixed space way station, a manned rocket around the moon and back, a manned landing on the moon and return, manned exploration of the planets and a fully controllable plane for space travel.

For any of the early items on this list, said the scientists, America's prospects for surpassing the Soviets were poor because of their initial rocket superiority. Our first best bet to beat them was the landing of a man on the moon.

The President was more convinced than any of his advisers that a second-rate, second-place space effort was inconsistent with this country's security, with its role as world leader and with the New Frontier spirit of discovery. Consequently he asked the Vice President as Chairman of the Space Council to seek answers to all the fundamental questions concerning the steps we could or must take to achieve pre-eminence in space—in terms of manpower, scientific talent, overtime facilities, alternative fuels, agency cooperation and money. Intensive hearings were held by the Council. The details of a new space budget were hammered out by Webb and McNamara. On the basis

A National Mission

Kennedy not only led America's space program, but on a larger scale, his leadership in space reflected the president's ability to capture the imagination of the American public.

For three years after 20 January 1961, the American people were persuaded that, metaphorically as well as literally, they could shoot for the moon. The language in which John Kennedy put forward his space programme was designed to excite a national will to conquer. "I believe that this nation should commit itself to achieving the goal, before this decade is out, of landing a man on the moon and returning him safely to earth," he said on 25 May 1961. "No single space project in this period will be more impressive to mankind. . . . In a very real sense, it will not be one man going to the moon; if we make this judgment affirmatively, it will be an entire nation. For all of us must work to put him there."

of these reports, the President made what he later termed one of the most important decisions he would make as President: "to shift our efforts in space from low to high gear." In his special second State of the Union Message of May, 1961, he included a determined and dramatic pledge: to land a man on the moon and return him safely to earth "before this decade is out."

"This Decade"

He was unwilling to promise a specific year, and referred to "this decade" as a deadline he could later interpret as either 1969 or 1970. James Webb, in fact, gave him visions of a late 1968 moon trip as a triumphant climax to his second term. (Under the level of support previously provided, the flight would not have been accomplished before the middle 1970's, if at all.) Whatever the date, the purpose of the

---

In fact, there was little that the majority of the American people could do to place a man on the moon, and there was no real way in which they could, as a nation, commit themselves to the task. The government of the United States was undertaking a scientific experiment; with the resources, tangible and intangible, at its disposal, there was little doubt that it would succeed. But this experiment was transformed into a national mission, and the national mission into a personal commitment on the part of countless individuals. The program could not succeed, he said, "unless every scientist, every engineer, every serviceman, every technician, contractor, and civil servant, gives his personal pledge that this nation will move forward, with the full speed of freedom, in the exciting adventure of space." The decision to shoot for the moon, in this kind of language, became a metaphor.

Henry Fairlie, *The Kennedy Promise: The Politics of Expectation.* Garden City, NY: Doubleday, 1973, pp. 12–13.

pledge was to provide a badly needed focus and sense of urgency for the entire space program. The lunar landing was not the sole space effort to be undertaken; but it was clearly one of the great human adventures of modern history.

"No single space project in this period," the President told the Congress, "will be more impressive to mankind or more important . . . [or] so difficult or expensive to accomplish." It would require, he said, the highest kind of national priority, the diversion of scientific manpower and funds from other important activities, a greater degree of dedication and discipline, and an end to all the petty stoppages, rivalries and personnel changes long troubling the space program.

> In a very real sense, it will not be one man going to the moon . . . it will be an entire nation. For all of us must work to put him there. . . . This is not merely a race. Space is open to us now; and our eagerness to share its meaning is not governed by the efforts of others. We go into space because whatever mankind must undertake, free men must fully share.

Congress and the Budget

The routine applause with which the Congress greeted this pledge struck him, he told me in the car going back to the White House, as something less than enthusiastic. Twenty billion dollars was a lot of money. The legislators knew a lot of better ways to spend it. Seated to the side of the rostrum, I thought the President looked strained in his effort to win them over. Suddenly he departed extensively from his prepared text—the only time he ever did that in addressing the Congress—to express his awareness of the responsibility they faced in making so expensive and long-range a commitment. "Unless we are prepared to do the work and bear the burdens to make it successful," he said, "there is no sense in going ahead." His voice sounded urgent but a little uncertain.

The Congress by nearly unanimous vote embraced what the President called this "great new American enterprise," aided by the successful shot of Commander Alan Shepard into space (although not into orbit) a few weeks earlier. The space budget was increased by 50 percent in that year. The following year it exceeded all the pre-1961 space budgets combined. Major new facilities sprang up in Houston, Texas, Cape Canaveral (now Cape Kennedy), Florida and elsewhere. Research produced for or from U.S. space launchings introduced advancements in dozens of other fields, ranging from medicine to metal fabrication. With the orbital flight of Colonel John Glenn in February, 1962, an instrumented flight past Venus later that year, and the use of a Telstar satellite to relay TV programs (including a Presidential news conference), the acceleration and expansion of America's space program began to gain ground.

The United States was still not first, said the President. . . . After each striking Soviet success, he noted, there were demands that we do more on a crash "Manhattan Project" basis. After each American astronaut's flight, there were demands that the world recognize our pre-eminence. But during the long intervals between flights, there were demands—sometimes from the same political and editorial sources—that our space budget be cut back and our timetable slowed down. Taxpayers complained about the cost. Scientists complained that more important activities were being slighted. Republicans began dipping into such phrases as "boondoggle" and "science fiction stunt."

But the President, once started, was not backing out. To those who said the money could better be spent relieving ignorance or poverty on this planet, he pointed out that this nation had the resources to do both but that those members of Congress making this point seemed unwilling to vote for more welfare funds, regardless of the size of the space program. To those who criticized concentration on the moon shot, he pointed out that this was a focal point for a broad-based scientific effort, and that some sixty other unrelated projects comprised nearly one-quarter of the space budget. To those who argued that instruments alone could do the job, he replied that man was "the most extraordinary computer of them all . . . [whose] judgment, nerve and . . . [ability to] learn from experience still make him unique" among the instruments. To those who feared that the publicity given our launchings would cost us heavily in the event of failure, he replied that this risk not only demonstrated our devotion to freedom but enhanced the prestige of successes which might otherwise be written off as second-best.

"A Man in Space"

He was concerned, to be sure, about risks to the astronauts' lives; and he made clear at the outset that, "Even if we should come in second . . . I will be satisfied if, when we finally put a man in space, his chances of survival are as high as I think they must be." He was also concerned about the program's effect on our nation's supply of scientists and engineers, and voiced new urgency for his higher education and other personnel development programs. He was concerned, finally, about waste and duplication in the space effort, and kept his Budget Director, Science Adviser and Space Council riding herd on the rapidly growing NASA complex (although not, he admitted, very successfully).

But he never relinquished that goal, "not simply to be first on the moon," as he put it, "any more than Charles Lindbergh's real aim was to be the first to Paris," but to strengthen our national leadership in a new and adventuresome age. In September of 1962, at Rice University in Houston, his most notable address on the subject summed up all the reasons why this nation must "set sail on this new sea." The exploration of space will go ahead whether we join it or not, he said; and just as the United States was founded by energy and vision, and achieved world leadership by riding the first waves of each new age—the industrial revolution, modern invention and nuclear power—so this generation of Americans intends to be "the world's leading space-faring nation." His remarks revealed much of his general outlook on life as well as on space:

> But why, some say, the moon? . . . And they may well ask, why climb the highest mountain? Why, thirty-five years ago, fly the Atlantic? Why does Rice play Texas? [A traditional, but almost inevitably more powerful, football rival.] . . .

> We choose to go to the moon in this decade, and do the other things, not because they are easy but because they are hard; because that goal will serve to organize and measure the best of our energies and skills. . . .

> Many years ago the great British explorer George Mallory, who was to die on Mount Everest, was asked why did he want to climb it, and he said, "Because it is there."

> Well, space is there, and . . . the moon and the planets are there, and new hopes for knowledge and peace are there.

A Turning Point and Progress

The Glenn flight [John Glenn reached orbit in 1962] was a turning point in many ways. Ten times it had been postponed. Frequently during the five-hour, three-orbit trip unforeseen dangers threatened to burn Glenn alive. The President, who enjoyed talking with each astronaut immediately upon the latter's safe return, personally liked Glenn immensely. Indeed, he found all the astronauts to be a remarkably competent and personable group. He did not approve of the rights granted them by his predecessor to make large profits through the exploitation of their names and stories while still in military service; nor did he want the period or frequency of their parades and speech making to reach a level interfering with their work. But he recognized that their courage and achievement merited special honors. "The impact of Colonel Glenn's magnificent achievement," he said, after Glenn was safely down, having watched his flight most of the day on TV, "goes far beyond our own time and our own country. We have a long way to go. We started late. But this is the new ocean, and I believe the United States must sail on it.". . .

The President's letter to Khrushchev on specific areas of cooperation largely repeated the proposals set forth over a year earlier in his first State of the Union: a joint weather satellite system, communications satellite coordination, an exchange of information on space medicine, cooperative tracking arrangements and other, less dramatic areas. The Soviet response was limited. Communist suspicions and secrecy were hard to dent, and negotiations proceeded slowly. Some of Kennedy's own advisers complained that too much cooperation instead of competition would dampen Congressional interest and appropriations. But the limited arrangement finally reached—and as of this writing never implemented by the Soviets—was at least a small first step toward fulfillment of the vow he made at Rice about space:

> . . . that we shall not see it governed by a hostile flag of conquest, but by a banner of freedom and peace . . . not . . . filled with weapons of mass destruction, but with instruments of knowledge and understanding . . . for the progress of all people.

Many Factors Shaped Kennedy's Space Policy

Donald W. Cox

Kennedy's call to the nation to put a man on the moon before the end of the decade was a far more complex decision than would appear. Indeed, critics have suggested that the president's stated goal was secondary to a number of other goals, including scientific progress, national security, and a global competition with communism to prove the superiority of democracy. It is even suggested that Kennedy's space race was an economic effort to create jobs, a politically motivated effort to deflect criticism from his poor handling of the Bay of Pigs invasion, and an expensive version of the old-fashioned military parade. Kennedy led an all out effort to reach the moon, marshaling resources, convincing skeptics, and capturing the imagination of the public. Donald W. Cox, a former lecturer and administrator with NASA and author of six books on space, asks readers to look deeper into the justification of the space race.

I N THE SPRING OF 1961, AFTER YURI GAGARIN HAD SETTLED the question of man's place in space, along with his ability to perform useful work there, President Kennedy was confronted with his first serious space problem after four months of indecision. The President's science advisers had been none too keen about manned spaceflight until some NASA and industry officials persuaded them, in the wake

Donald W. Cox, "Our Grand Assault on the Moon," *The Space Race: From Sputnik to Apollo . . . and Beyond.* New York: Chilton Books, 1962.

of the *Vostok I*, that the United States had all the engineering knowledge and ability to send men to the moon as early as 1967. No big "breakthrough" in fuels, boosters, or guidance equipment was needed, they assured the White House.

Dr. Jerome Wiesner, the President's scientific adviser, and budget director David Bell carried this information to the President. On May 25, President Kennedy went before a special joint session of Congress and asked that the idea of putting men on the moon be taken from the realm of science fiction and made into national policy for the United States. "No single space project . . . will be more exciting or more impressive or more important for the long-range exploration of space," the President said, "and none will be so difficult or expensive." He made clear that it was his judgment that it would be worth the effort and the cost. The President then requested a sharp step-up in funds to support this effort, beginning in the fiscal year starting on July 1, with an additional seven to nine billion dollars over the next five years.

More important than the cold figures of the budgetary increase, however, was the President's emphatic policy declaration, made at the end of his address, that the nation should now commit itself to "a great new American enterprise" of attempting to land a man on the moon and return him safely to earth before the end of the decade. He made it clear that this national goal was "not merely a race of getting to the moon ahead of Russia" and that our eagerness to share space's meaning was "not governed by the efforts of others, but by our unquenchable thirst for the exploration of the unknown characteristic of the spirit of free men throughout history—and by our eagerness to advance scientific knowledge. . . . We go into space because whatever mankind must undertake, free men must fully share."

Although he conceded that there was an element of a race involved in putting the first man on the moon, it was made secondary to the main purpose of meeting the challenge with all the intellectual, material, and spiritual resources at our command. The President warned his audience that, while we could not guarantee that we should one day be first, "we can guarantee that any failure to share this effort will make us last." He cautioned his listeners that we should not become embroiled in a crash moon program, since there is "one purpose that this nation will never overlook—the survival of the man who makes this first daring flight."

One reason for the long delay in reaching this momentous White House space decision was the controversy that had brewed within the new Administration over the wisdom of spending a figure almost equal to an entire year's national defense budget to reach the moon. The running debate between many scientists and government officials—including some on the President's science advisory committee—witnessed many strong arguments in favor of a more profitable spending of that enormous amount of money on more scientific research and education here on earth instead.

During the early months of his Administration, President Kennedy seemed to have been largely influenced by these non-space scientists when he rejected a $182,521,000 supplemental request for additional NASA funds by the space agency in March, some of which would have gone for our man-in-space projects. He had even cautioned against rushing into a man-on-the-moon project in late April "until we really know where we are going to end up." Even in the face of Major Gagarin's epic-making orbital flight in April, he still had continued to suggest that the United States should perhaps concentrate its money in other areas of research "where we can be first and will bring perhaps more long-range benefits to mankind."

His predecessor, President Eisenhower, had shackled NASA with a document which prevented the agency from going beyond Project *Mercury* with manned spaceflight.

This rule was still in force up until May 25 when President Kennedy accompanied his second message to Congress with a restoration of the stricken space funds plus a half-billion more dollars, as the first installment on an accelerated effort that would add some $9,000,000,000 to the cost of the space program in the next few years. This major step forward in space meant that the U.S. would be spending at least $30,000,000,000 during the 1961–66 period on the civilian and military exploration of space. Eisenhower called this new program "a mad effort to win a stunt race."

"A Foolish Waste of Money"

Some congressmen took a dim view of the special moon message, particularly its over-all cost. Representative Clarence Cannon, D., Mo., chairman of the House Appropriations Committee, demanded that the White House abandon or scale down this spectacular lunar undertaking. In a meeting with the President at the White House a few days later, the eighty-two-year-old Cannon challenged the wisdom of such lavish spending on a crash space program. In his private talk with President Kennedy, Representative Cannon took the frank position that he couldn't support the moon project because it would be "a fantastic, foolish waste of money."

"This country shouldn't pour billions of dollars down the rat-hole of space just to try to regain international prestige," Cannon told the President. "That prestige was lost for good when Russia put the first man in space. It can't be recaptured by spending billions more."

The President disagreed with the Congressman, reiterating the highlights of his message to Congress on the subject. Cannon then countered that the nine billion dollars was a "scientific luxury," and should be abandoned "so that it will not divert our national effort from more urgent defense challenges here on earth."

The President then cordially inquired of his guest, "What

do you think we should be doing that we aren't doing now?"

Cannon thundered back that "we should be spending these billions on improving our military striking power to deter Russia from taking over the earth. It isn't going to do us any good to land on the moon if we let Khrushchev get a military advantage over us. I for one do not believe that he is bluffing when he says he will try to bury us."

"Neither do I!" responded the President immediately. He

Astronauts Edwin "Buzz" Aldrin (shown here) and Neil Armstrong landed on the moon in 1969. Kennedy wanted to land an American astronaut on the moon by the end of the 1960s.

then tried once more to stress the dual importance to our national security of both a strong military posture and of ensuring that the first man on the moon was from America.

The meeting ended with neither the President nor Cannon making a convert of the other.

Democracy vs. Communism

Few people knew that the President had actually embarked on an educational gamble to prove the merits of Democracy vs. Communism when he made his man-on-the-moon plea to Congress, since a Gallup Poll taken just before his message showed that only one American in three was in favor of a major lunar program. This poll was based on the estimated cost of $40,000,000,000 or $225 per person to send a man to the moon.

Why had the President suddenly made this momentous decision that signaled such a definite shift in American policy on spaceflight? Many people believed that the President chose to take a short cut to the moon, not because of any overriding military necessity of establishing a moon base there ahead of the Soviets, nor because of any pressing lunar scientific research that had to be conducted at the moment. The American scientific community had several other choices of higher priority projects on which to spend such vast sums of money rather than an all-out crash program of putting one man on the moon by 1967.

What then was the real reason behind the President's decision to move ahead on the last frontier? Most close observers of the Washington scene felt that his unannounced motivation for plunging into the manned lunar race could be found mainly in the political sphere. What better escape from the trauma of the Cuban invasion fiasco than to focus the public's attention on a journey to the moon?

Since we were just beginning to shake our way out of the economic recession of 1960, the job opportunities of an expanded civilian space program especially in the fields of rocket technology offered the Administration a promising source for more work. In a sense, the rocket industries had been taking up the major job slack left in the wake of the decline in business sustained by the older aircraft industries of World War II days.

Rationale for the Voyage

The closest approach that any responsible scientist made to explain the President's space views in public occurred at a special symposium conducted by the Washington [D.C.] Academy of Sciences during the summer of 1961. The spokesman was none other than Dr. Lloyd Berkner, chairman of the Space Science Board of the Academy, founder of the IGY, and top consultant to the President's science advisory committee. Dr. Berkner drew an analogy between Mr. Kennedy's recent proposal to race the Russians to the moon and the policy of bread and circuses that kept the peace for so long in ancient Rome. In short—a race to the moon would be a worthwhile substitute for a shooting war here on earth.

Dr. Berkner also stressed the foreign policy justification for going to the moon, in that such a successful voyage would demonstrate American "technological flexibility" and reassert our lost prestige in the eyes of the rest of the world. This feat would be a modern-day substitute for the old-fashioned terrestrial military parade—with the resulting space fireworks being safer but just as spectacular as exploding hydrogen bombs.

There was considerable feeling in Washington that we could win the race to the moon by brute force if we could only mobilize our industry as we did against Hitler and the Japanese in another era. Without superior industrial capacity, it was felt that if we could put it to work at the proper pace we could then show the uncommitted nations of the world who had the stronger house in which to lodge a friend—the White House or the Kremlin.

CHAPTER

5

MANAGING
THE PRESS

Kennedy's Style Was Suited to Television

Mary Ann Watson

Kennedy's style fit well with the new visual medium. Indeed, he came to define and dominate the relationship between politics and television. Kennedy understood the power of television and this is most apparent in the famous Nixon-Kennedy debate, the first nationally televised presidential debate, held in Chicago on September 26, 1960. Mary Ann Watson, a professor of communication at the University of Michigan, reveals the actions and decisions by Kennedy and his aides behind the scenes during the 1960 campaign and the "Great Debate" to ensure that the candidate was presented in the most positive light.

I T IS IMPOSSIBLE TO SEPARATE THE MAJOR EVENTS OF AMERI-can history in the early 1960s from the development of American television. They are inextricably intertwined. The Kennedy years stand out as an era bracketed by TV milestones. In the years between the Great Debates and the network coverage of the assassination and funeral of the President, television became truly central to American life.

The New Frontier was a time in which traditions were being established in the young medium. Its resonance has not yet faded. It was a time when our broadcast heritage was emerging. Viewing patterns would be set; fundamentals of TV production ordained.

Mary Ann Watson, *The Expanding Vista: American Television in the Kennedy Years.* New York: Oxford University Press, 1990. Copyright © 1990 by Mary Ann Watson. Reproduced by permission of Oxford University Press, Inc.

John Kennedy's overriding campaign theme in 1960 was the need "to get America moving again." After the seeming stillness of the Eisenhower years, the promise of a society in motion, however vague, was exhilarating. And television, itself making technological strides, was the perfect medium to chronicle movement. But the currents of change would be stronger and swifter than anyone could have imagined.

A New Medium for a New Type of Politician

During the Kennedy years, so crowded with occurrences of critical consequence, television kept pace in a way that newspapers and magazines could not. Radio's inability to convey the images of motion rendered it incapable of adequately capturing the temper of the times. The dynamics of the era propelled television's development and, in turn, the force of the medium shaped the social landscape. . . .

The presidential election of 1960 was to be a barometer of a new era. It represented a shift in American political technique and underscored the forcefulness of television in the formation of public opinion. . . .

By 1956 John Kennedy, who had already made a rapid rise in national politics, was growing more aware of the danger in underestimating the magnitude of the medium and the benefits of catering to it. His TV appearances in the early 1950s on news panel discussion shows, such as *Meet the Press*, while not flawless, displayed enviable ease. In October 1953, shortly after his highly publicized high-society wedding, Senator Kennedy and his bride were on Edward R. Murrow's *Person to Person*, a live interview program broadcast, in part, from the homes of the guests. The conversation could charitably be referred to as stilted, which, in many ways, was a hallmark of the times and the series. . . .

Kennedy was one of several men Stevenson was considering for his running mate in 1956. The nominee decided, however, to let the convention select the vice-presidential candidate. It was Senator Kennedy's good fortune to narrowly lose the vice-presidential nomination to Senator Estes Kefauver of Tennessee, which meant Kennedy escaped any blame for Stevenson's loss to Eisenhower. He was remembered instead for his delivery of the speech nominating Stevenson. It transfigured Kennedy into the party's brightest star. Television viewers were favorably impressed with the slender and winsome senator from Massachusetts. He was very soon the most sought after speaker in the Democratic party and clearly a strong contender for 1960. . . .

The readers of *TV Guide* found the by-line of Senator John F. Kennedy in the magazine's November 14, 1959, issue. In his article, "A Force That Has Changed the Political Scene," he gracefully anticipated some of the criticism that would be directed his way in the following year. Television image, he argued, is not simply a counterfeit measure of a candidate's capacity to govern and lead. Rather, it is a substantive factor. "Honesty, vigor, compassion, intelligence—the presence or lack of these and other qualities make up what is called the candidate's 'image,'" he wrote. "My own conviction is that these images or impressions are likely to be uncannily correct."

Television and the Campaign

On January 2, 1960, John Kennedy formally announced what even the most casual observer already knew was fact—he was running for the Democratic presidential nomination. The following day he appeared on *Meet the Press* and made it very clear he would not settle for the vice-presidential spot. In 1960, he said, the American public would "presume that the presidential candidate is going to have a normal life expectancy." He felt, therefore, the second name on the ticket was not going to be of critical importance to American voters. Kennedy said he was not interested in spending the next eight years of his life "breaking ties (in the Senate) and waiting for the president to die."

As the 1960 primary season unfolded, Kennedy's

Catholicism promised to be a damaging circumstance. The West Virginia primary was the turning point on the issue. And it was a television appearance that was the turning point in the primary.

Against the advice of many seasoned politicians, the candidate decided to confront religious prejudice straightaway instead of sidestepping it. For almost two weeks before the vote in West Virginia, Kennedy boldly and emotionally referred to his religion in personal appearances. "Nobody asked me if I was Catholic when I joined the United States Navy," he said. "And nobody asked my brother if he was Catholic or Protestant before he climbed into an American bomber plane to fly his last mission."

The Sunday before election day, the Kennedy cam-

The Kennedy Style

Historian James David Barber writes that Kennedy's ease with the media and his successful style were the result of his character.

His manner was quiet, factual, direct, and increasingly confident as he quickly became an old hand at approaching people. His speechmaking, halting at first, gained power: "He slowly developed a style of direct, informal, simple speaking, without high-blown rhetoric or bombastic exaggeration, that to some of his listeners was in happy contrast to the oratory of the old-fashioned politicians," Burns says. Yet he found he could also call occasionally on the Fitzgerald in him. Once, at a rally, when he was making a strong speech for veteran's housing, an old Irishman named Jackie Toomey queried, "What about the *non*-veteran?" Jack snapped back with "Yes, sir, the *non*-veteran too." After the meeting a smiling Jackie Toomey circulated among the crowd saying, "You see—he's for the non-veteran too." Kennedy also learned to speak toughly. At another rally the WAC major, in her white

paign purchased thirty minutes of television time. The format of the discussion program had Franklin Roosevelt, Jr., asking the questions the candidate would answer. Within the first few minutes of the program, as planned, the question of religion was raised. Kennedy did not direct his answer to Roosevelt or focus on him. He looked directly into the lens of the camera, into the eyes of the voters, as he delivered an impassioned statement of principle on the separation of church and state. He was deeply persuasive.

Kennedy had been trailing Hubert Humphrey—who had a far more active Senate record—in the polls throughout the primary, though he was gaining momentum. Following the Sunday night program Kennedy took a slim lead. When Tuesday's votes were counted, though, the

---

uniform, gave him a public raking-over and then whispered to him, "Don't pay any attention—it's just politics." When Kennedy's turn came he gave a harsh counterattack. . . .

There was not a great deal of talk about "style" in politics before the Kennedys. The campaign had an elan, a dash and flair, flowing outward from the brave-young-candidate to his audiences. People saw in him what they wanted to: the Irish lad made good, the crisp Harvard mind, the battle-scarred veteran, the scion of unfathomable wealth, the handsome, humble fellow destined for mysterious greatness. Whatever it was, it added up to charisma, a pawed-over concept Kennedy brought back to clarity. For all his apparent modesty—perhaps in part *because* of that—Jack left people feeling they could do better and enjoy it. Even then, Kennedy and the Kennedys went around enspiriting people, calling forth their hope.

James David Barber, *The Presidential Character: Predicting Performance in the White House.* Englewood Cliffs, NJ: Prentice-Hall, 1992, pp. 356–57.

Massachusetts senator's victory in West Virginia was not even a close call. He captured more than 60 percent of the vote. Later, during the general election, network television's generous coverage of Kennedy's eloquent remarks on religion addressed to the Greater Houston Ministerial Association finally put the matter to rest.

Personality Politics

Kennedy's polished use of television in West Virginia was enhanced by the ineptitude and naivete of his opponent. Humphrey foolishly challenged Kennedy to a televised debate, resulting in the senator from Minnesota being upstaged by Kennedy's aplomb. Both candidates shared similar views on the federal government's responsibility to the impoverished families of West Virginia. Kennedy, however, brought with him to the TV studio a government-distributed food package that included the daily ration of powdered milk made available to the unemployed poor. He *visually* underscored his concern. . . .

John Kennedy believed that nonpolitical talk to the unconvinced was better than political talk to the already convinced. Television expedited the impact of his logic. His appearance on Jack Paar's *Tonight Show* in June 1960 demonstrated Kennedy's ability and willingness to use TV for personality projection.

In Paar's introduction of the candidate, he welcomed him to the "relaxed atmosphere" of the late-night talk show and said, "I think Mr. Kennedy came here tonight because he feels he can reach people who would not ordinarily watch news programs." Their conversation, which included actress Anne Bancroft and comedienne Peggy Cass, was pleasantly jocular. Kennedy seemed altogether accessible.

At the first commercial break, Paar deferentially apologized for the interruption, but Kennedy responded, "No, don't apologize—that's how it all operates." When telling a campaign anecdote, Kennedy alluded to the many popular prime-time western series on the air. As the lengthy interview came to a close, Kennedy told Paar, "In campaigning through Wisconsin and West Virginia I ran into a lot of people who sat up nights watching you. And I think anytime it's possible for those of us in public life to have a chance to communicate, I think we ought to take it. Therefore, I regard it as a privilege to appear on this program.". . .

Rewriting the Campaign Book

From Labor Day to election day, Kennedy adhered to a relentless schedule of personal appearances, with an emphasis on swing states, fully aware of the dividends of local and national television coverage. An associate professor of voice and speech at Boston University—a former opera singer—was retained to help the candidate maintain his vocal timbre through relaxation techniques used by professional performers.

His campaign also secured the services of a new kind of business, Mobile Video Tapes, to record every stop in its entirety. The idea of video documentation was an appealing one to Kennedy. It was not as important to the Nixon team, though. The company received no reply from the Republicans when it offered the same videotaping service.

As a candidate, and later as president, Kennedy shunned silly hats and kissing babies. Looking presidential mattered. Kennedy also jettisoned conventional wisdom about the rhetoric of campaign stumping. He didn't make homespun references to the town he was in or pretend to be interested in the winning season of the local football team. His hand waves of greeting were tentative, rarely above shoulder height. Kennedy held back; he didn't give himself to a crowd. He was in control even when passionate. On television, a medium that magnifies personalities and mannerisms, Kennedy's reserve translated into a dignified, statesmanlike persona. . . .

Nixon vs. Kennedy: The Great Debate

All three networks extended formal invitations to the candidates, though NBC was the first. The very night Nixon was nominated, Chairman of the Board Robert Sarnoff sent wires to the two men. Sarnoff is credited with coining the title "The Great Debates" in his invitation.

Kennedy accepted without hesitation. He had everything to gain. The debates would magnify his status and would be his best chance to close the "maturity gap," the lingering perception that the senator was simply too young and inexperienced for the position he sought.

A week before the first debate, on the CBS program *Presidential Countdown: Mr. Kennedy, A Profile*, Walter Cronkite asked the candidate, "Do you ever wish that you looked older?" Kennedy believed his youthfulness would ultimately work to his advantage. Concerning Kennedy's hairstyle, the reporter asked if "getting away from the forelock" was "a considered political opinion." "Well," Senator Kennedy replied with good-natured irritation, "I've been cutting it the same way for six or seven years—or even longer. But, it's a—unfortunately when you run for the presidency, your wife's hair or your hair or something else always becomes of major significance. I don't think it's the great issue, though, in 1960."

Nixon had more to lose than to gain by participating in the debates. He was urged by many, including President Eisenhower, to avoid a forum that would put Kennedy on seemingly equal footing. But the prospect of looking like he was chickening out of a fair fight was unacceptable to the vice-president. It was a matter of personal pride.

The logistics and the debate formats were sorted out in careful negotiations, fifteen meetings in all, among the networks and representatives of the candidates. By mid September all parties had agreed to four one-hour programs that would air simultaneously on all three television networks and all four radio networks. In precise terms, the joint appearances were not debates; they were closer to news conferences. Nevertheless, the coverage was focused on the idea that there would be a winner and a loser. . . .

No Contest

A myriad of factors converged that evening for a hapless Richard Nixon. Not yet completely recovered from his serious and painful hospital stay, his wan appearance looked even worse when juxtaposed with Kennedy's suntanned countenance. This, of course, was beyond Nixon's control, but Nixon was less aggressive than Kennedy in controlling what he could.

Kennedy displayed greater astuteness about the process of television production and paid closer attention to detail. The day before the first debate Kennedy himself and his broadcast strategist, J. Leonard Reinsch, met with Don Hewitt, the CBS director of the telecast, to discuss set design and shooting patterns. The same invitation was extended to Nixon but was not accepted. The vice-president declined the valuable opportunity to familiarize himself with the venue of a performance that would be critical for him.

The day of the first debate, Kennedy kept a light schedule, only a short meeting at noon with a labor group. The rest of that Monday was spent studying, with the phone off the hook, from a stack of index cards and a notebook labelled "What Nixon Said." After dinner he took a short nap. It was going to be a big night.

The dramatic tension of the first debate was enhanced by the latest Gallup poll, which indicated an even split of 47 percent of the electorate for each man, with 6 percent of the voters undecided. A hint of true acrimony between the candidates added interest.

Both candidates were offered the services of a professional make-up artist brought in by the network from New York. Both refused. Kennedy needed no make-up. Nixon did, but he was touched up questionably by a member of his own staff. It was a regrettable folly that has become a permanent footnote in American political history.

When the studio lights were being checked shortly before airtime, Hewitt commented that Kennedy's white shirt caused an unattractive glare. An aide to the senator was promptly sent to bring one of Kennedy's blue shirts back to the station. Combined with his dark blue suit, Kennedy would look crisp and stand out from the neutral gray background. In comparison, Nixon's recent eight-pound weight loss caused his shirt collar to sag ever so slightly and his light gray suit blended blandly into the set.

Moments before air Robert Kennedy was looking at the image of the candidates on the monitor. He was surprised at Nixon's peaked appearance. When Nixon spotted him checking the screen, he asked what the younger Kennedy thought. "Dick," the candidate's brother said, "you look great."

Image

Throughout the campaign, and especially in regard to the debates, John Kennedy sought out and respected the expertise of media professionals. Nixon had savvy media advisors on his staff and at his disposal as well, but he did not make good use of their knowledge. Nixon's style was insular. He dismissed the advice of men who had impressive credentials and track records in the broadcast media. He misjudged what mattered most.

Whether or not Nixon and Kennedy were substantively peers that evening—as the research on the radio audience indicates they were—hardly mattered. It was the combination of sight and sound that determined the winner. And Kennedy outdistanced the vice-president by furlongs. . . .

Russell Baker, covering the story for *The New York Times*, recalled listening to but not watching a TV monitor at the Chicago studio: "I thought Nixon had a slight edge in what little argument there had been but as I talked to more and more people it was clear they thought Kennedy had won a great victory. . . . I missed it completely because I had been too busy taking notes and writing to get more than fleeting glimpses of what the country was seeing on the screen. That night television replaced newspapers as the most important communications medium in American politics."

In the days that followed, Kennedy's crowds grew noisier and television's critics quieter. The medium emerged with a greater aura of respectability. Television also became a bigger part of the story of the campaign. Through standard news reports the public was getting acquainted with the behind-the-scenes considerations of television. The fact that television mediated reality was discussed not only in college classrooms, but around the office water cooler and over the back fence. . . .

J. Leonard Reinsch believed the vice-president was a "psychosomatic sweater." Nixon's visible perspiration in the reaction shots of the first debate delighted Reinsch since the Republican candidate's perceived nervousness could only reflect favorably on Kennedy. It was just the kind of television image he had hoped for. . . .

Triumph on Television

The significance of television in the outcome of the election became the subject of wide discussion in the mass media. Most people came to the same conclusion the president-elect did—television was indeed the edge in his narrow margin of victory. And J. Leonard Reinsch was heralded as "the architect of a triumph on television."

"Kennedy happens to look like a composite picture of all the good stereotypes television has created," wrote one political science professor in his assessment of Campaign '60. And, as one senior citizen told an interviewer conducting survey research on the campaign for the University of Michigan, she did not vote for Nixon because she "didn't like the look in his eyes—especially the left one." . . .

The transition from the Eisenhower administration to the New Frontier unfolded on TV screens everywhere as JFK's every move was followed. The television networks competed to cover the Kennedy Inaugural and associated events in the most spectacular, and at the same time, most intimate way. In the fifteen hours between his attendance at morning Mass and his leaving the Inaugural Ball, TV technicians scrambled in the snow along with secret service agents to keep up with the indefatigable John Kennedy.

A lover of poetry, Kennedy understood symbolism. He wanted to use, in the words of British journalist Henry Fairlie, "images of excellence to adorn his Presidency." And he did so exquisitely on the first day. The cultural sheen of his Inaugural was meant to be a harbinger of an uplifting of the American social imagination.

It was a day of striking imagery. The touching sight of Robert Frost blinded by the glare of the sun as he attempted to read from his manuscript; the reserve of Kennedy's wife and the exuberance of his sisters; the gracious and familiar smile of a now former president who suddenly looked old.

Television pictures provided a wonderfully paradoxical portrait of President Kennedy. He was both exalted and personalized. It was the new leader of the free world who punctuated the lofty rhetoric of his inaugural address with emphatic hand motions and pointed finger; but it was a regular kind of guy who got caught running a pocket comb through his generously endowed head of hair when he thought no one was looking.

The New Frontier was off and running, but television would do more than simply follow dizzily from the speed. An unspoken alliance had been formed, a symbiotic bond between Kennedy and the medium. The telegenic new President's affinity for television was going to alter the nature of the relationship between the public and the chief executive. It was also going to define the nature of the relationship between the chief executive and the medium.

Kennedy's Relations with the Press Were Not Always Smooth

Charles Lam Markmann and Mark Sherwin

John F. Kennedy ushered in a new approach to working with the press. Woodrow Wilson was the first to use press conferences for political gain, and Franklin Roosevelt mastered the press conference with his confident style and rapport with the American public. Yet, Kennedy brought energy, charisma, and a deep understanding of both the press and publicity to the presidency. Kennedy's ability to manage the press changed presidential-press relations and benefited his presidency, yet this relationship was not always as positive as it has often been described. Some members of the press corps were aware of Kennedy's efforts at "news management," while others resented his stifling of free and open reporting. Charles Lam Markmann and Mark Sherwin have both published on American politics and were among the first to produce a biography of President Kennedy.

D URING THE CAMPAIGN, KENNEDY'S FORCEFUL, ENERGETIC personality on television had won to his cause many doubters and reluctant voters. Therefore it was natural that his first television press conference should draw an enviably large audience. One week after he took office, Kennedy stood on the rostrum in the spacious auditorium of the

Charles Lam Markmann and Mark Sherwin, *John F. Kennedy: A Sense of Purpose*. New York: St. Martin's Press, 1961.

new State Department Building facing 418 news men, a record attendance. He set the pattern by opening with a statement—the most startling ever made at a press conference. He announced: "Captains Freeman B. Olmstead and John R. McKone, members of the crew of the U.S.A.F. RB-47 aircraft who have been detained by Soviet authorities since July 1, 1960, have been released by the Soviet Government and are now en route to the United States." When the excitement had subsided, he continued with discussions of other plans, speaking quietly, incisively and clearly. Then he answered 31 questions in 38 minutes, impressing the reporters and his television audience with his knowledge of all matters that came up for discussion. He used his right arm in a waving motion as if to put punctuation and emphasis to his replies. The news men were visibly impressed and the viewers at home were enthralled and enchanted with a President who seemed to know all the answers. And the intellectuals were delighted with a President who understood syntax and spoke in sentences.

Kennedy and the Press

As the news conferences on television continued, always beginning with announcements and statements from the President, the veteran reporters examined this new method and found several flaws. Aside from the fact that the conference lacked the give-and-take atmosphere of Roosevelt's and Truman's sessions, there was a growing resentment that the announcements shrank the time left for questions in the traditional 30 minutes. Since it was impolite to break into a discussion while millions watched, reporters suffered the unhappy feeling that Kennedy was using the haphazard method of selecting his questioners to play favorites. The President was not at fault alone. Criticism was leveled at reporters who used the television scanners in the interest of publicizing themselves and asking trivial and unanswerable questions; for example: "Would you wel-

Kennedy's popularity was bolstered by his uncanny ability to manipulate the press. The public responded enthusiastically to his press conferences.

come a visit from Mr. Khrushchev in the next few weeks or months?" "Do you propose to spark from the White House the one-man movement started by a Republican relative of yours in Oklahoma to restore the sound dollar?" (The Republican was no relative.) "Have you determined whether any in the State Department helped to advance the Communist foothold in Cuba, and if so will you take steps to remove them from office?" The President managed to answer these and many other silly questions with poise and patience. And he impressed his listeners with his exact knowledge of a molasses shipment from Cuba and several other matters that appeared as if the questioner had specifically copied some obscure figures for the sake of demonstrating his erudition.

Nevertheless, the televised press conference served Kennedy well. Arthur Krock wrote in *The Times:*

> In this revitalized atmosphere of government by a Chief Executive who has an intelligent and tireless interest in its over-all and detailed functioning, the White House news conferences themselves have become even more the instrument of the President. The questions grow fewer because Mr. Kennedy has employed them more as a platform to make important announcements of acts and policies. Through the projection of television, live or canned, this expansion of the President's role has well served the dual purpose of informing the United States and the world on vital and timely matters and providing him with a better forum than has been built on that foundation before. And that is one of the most effective means of transmitting to the furthest reaches of the planet an impression of new vitality in Washington.

Appealing to the Public

Kennedy's intense desire to arouse the people from their apathy of the "Easy Fifties" and to cast a brighter light in broad areas of ignorance showed some gratifying results. While the public-opinion polls indicated his popularity was growing in a rather casual way, other statistics were even more heartening. The White House switchboard was 60 per cent busier than it was before Kennedy took office; mail arrived at the rate of 30,000 letters a week, and the same general attitude of awakening was reflected in the phone calls and mail received by Cabinet members. Yet there was the grave concern that the vibrant New Frontier might wear out its welcome with the easily distracted mass of television viewers who could retreat to their cowboy or gangster violence and just say: "Let Jack do it."

The President repeatedly told the people that the world

looked to the United States for leadership despite Communist propaganda; that our leadership depended largely upon an informed electorate, and that no Administration could succeed if the country did not understand. He was openly disturbed by reports that only three in ten voters were aware of the major problems in foreign affairs and that two in ten could be considered reasonably well informed. In defense of this state of affairs it was noted that never before in the history of this nation had its foreign affairs been so perplexing, so varied and so complicated. The tones and shadings became increasingly confusing. The ordinary citizen could not understand why tiny Laos, so far away, was important. He had been conditioned by the films and television to understand the difference between the good guy and the bad guy. He felt secure in the single knowledge that Communism was the bad guy, Uncle Sam was the good guy. As for the rest, it was up to the man who was President.

In striving for the greater dissemination of information, Kennedy indicated that what we do not know is certain to hurt us. These words were to come back in a different light when he addressed the American Newspaper Publishers' Association in New York. He began gently by asking the publishers to reconsider the meaning of freedom of the press. Then he outlined the "distinct" advantages that a closed totalitarian society held over an open society. "Its preparations," he said of the closed society, "are concealed, not published. Its mistakes are buried, not headlined . . . No expenditure is questioned, no rumor is printed, no secret is revealed. It conducts the cold war, in short, with a wartime discipline no democracy could ever hope—or wish—to match."

Politics, the Press, and Bias

The President went on to show that every democracy recognized the necessary restraints of national security—

"and the question remains whether those restraints need to be more strictly observed if we are to oppose this kind of attack as well as outright invasion." He declared that this nation's foes had openly boasted of acquiring through American newspapers information they would otherwise hire agents to acquire through theft, bribery or espionage. "Details of this nation's covert preparations," he said, "to counter the enemy's covert operations have been available to every newspaper reader, friend and foe alike." He pointed out that the size, strength, the location and nature of our forces and weapons, and our plans and strategy for their use, had all been pinpointed in the press and other news media to a degree sufficient to satisfy any foreign power; and that, in at least one case, the publication of details concerning a secret mechanism by which satellites were followed required its alteration at the expense of considerable time and money.

"The newspapers which printed these stories," he said, "were loyal, patriotic, responsible and well-meaning. Had we been engaged in open warfare, they undoubtedly would not have published such items. But in the absence of open warfare, they recognized only the tests of journalism and not the tests of national security. And my question . . . is whether additional tests should not now be adopted. That question is for you alone to answer.

"I have no intention of establishing a new Office of War Information to govern the flow of news. I am not suggesting any new forms of censorship or new types of security classifications. I have no easy answer to the dilemma I have posed, and I would not seek to impose it if I had one. But I am asking the members of the newspaper profession and the industry in this country to re-examine their own responsibilities—to consider the degree and the nature of the present danger—and to heed the duty of self restraint which that danger imposes upon us all.

"Every newspaper now asks itself, with respect to every

story: 'Is it news?' All I suggest is that you add the question: 'Is it in the interest of national security?' And I hope that every group in America—unions and business men and public officials at every level—will ask the same question of their endeavors, and subject their actions to this same exacting test.

"And should the press of America consider and recommend the voluntary assumption of specific new steps or machinery, I can assure you that we will cooperate wholeheartedly with those recommendations."

The President made clear to the publishers that he had no desire to stifle controversy or criticism, and that his Administration intended to be candid about its errors. . . .

The Reaction

The reaction was as expected from a press traditionally suspicious of any move to control it—even benevolently.

"There is no need for further restrictive machinery," said the *New York Herald Tribune.* "In days of peril especially, the country needs more facts, not fewer. In the long run, competent, thorough and aggressive news reporting is the uncompromising servant of the national interest— even though it may be momentarily embarrassing to the Government."

The *Portland Oregonian* made the point that what is needed "far more is discipline among government officials, both civilian and military; first, to keep the people properly informed; second, to guard legitimate secrets from leaks, lies, misinterpretation and inter-agency sabotage." The *Newark Evening News* asked who was to define the national interest. "The press believes the public's right to know is a fundamental of democratic government. But where does this right collide with national security? If Mr. Kennedy . . . can tell us, he will not find the press uncooperative."

If Kennedy intended to enter into debate with the editorial writers, he did not get the immediate opportunity because at this time the Cuban adventure exploded all over the front pages, keeping him and his press secretary fully occupied. Salinger himself was nursing wounds suffered at a panel session of the American Society of Newspaper Editors where Peter Lisagor, Washington bureau chief of the Chicago *Daily News,* had finally openly voiced the complaint that reporters were "little more than props for the TV press conference." Lisagor and others said it would "be nice to know when the Irish temper behind the Harvard façade had been excited. This could be accomplished by sitting a little closer to the President." The normally good-humored Salinger replied rather testily that "people who long for the good old days of F.D.R. are unrealistic. Television is here to stay." It was only natural that Salinger should be subject to comparison with his predecessor. White House correspondents felt that Salinger had not yet achieved "the polish and sure-footedness of Hagerty;" that he properly spoke less for Kennedy than Hagerty did for Eisenhower; that he often ignored telephone calls; that he was frequently late in holding his twice-a-day press briefings and that he was often not certain of his information. But all agreed that "Plucky Pierre," as he was sometimes called behind his ample back, did a prodigious amount of work, was willing to admit errors and definitely made no attempt to create a wall around the President. Salinger's own appraisal of his work so far was: "I think the people are getting a closer view of the President than they've ever had—and that's just what we want."

"The More Popular I Get"

The closer view evidently favored Kennedy, as private and public polls showed an ever-increasing popularity and, what was even more encouraging, a genuine sympathy for his burdens of office. He made it a practice on some quiet weekend afternoons, rare though they were, to walk into the press room, which is really a large anteroom to the executive offices, and have a casual chat with reporters. Such visits were generally not mentioned and definitely were not to be construed as any form of press conference, briefing or background session. Shortly after the Cuban mishap, someone remarked that the Gallup Poll indicated that his popularity had reached a new peak. "My God," he exclaimed, "it's as bad as Eisenhower. The worse I do, the more popular I get."

Appendix of Documents

Document 1: Announcing His Candidacy for President

Kennedy began his presidential campaign early, delivering a short announcement on January 2, 1960, in the U.S. Senate Caucus Room in the Capitol.

I am announcing today my candidacy for the Presidency of the United States.

The Presidency is the most powerful office in the Free World. Through its leadership can come a more vital life for our people. In it are centered the hopes of the globe around us for freedom and a more secure life. For it is in the Executive Branch that the most crucial decisions of this century must be made in the next four years—how to end or alter the burdensome arms race, where Soviet gains already threaten our very existence—how to maintain freedom and order in the newly emerging nations—how to rebuild the stature of American science and education—how to prevent the collapse of our farm economy and the decay of our cities—how to achieve, without further inflation or unemployment, expanded economic growth benefiting all Americans—and how to give direction to our traditional moral purpose, awakening every American to the dangers and opportunities that confront us.

These are among the real issues of 1960. And it is on the basis of these issues that the American people must make their fateful choice for their future.

In the past 40 months, I have toured every state in the Union and I have talked to Democrats in all walks of life. My candidacy is therefore based on the conviction that I can win both the nomination and the election.

I believe that any Democratic aspirant to this important nomination should be willing to submit to the voters his views, record and competence in a series of primary contests. I am therefore now announcing my intention of filing in the New Hampshire primary and I shall announce my plans with respect to the other primaries as their filing dates approach.

I believe that the Democratic Party has a historic function to perform in the winning of the 1960 election, comparable to its role in 1932. I intend to do my utmost to see that that victory is won.

For 18 years, I have been in the service of the United States, first as a naval officer in the Pacific during World War II and for the past 14 years as a member of the Congress. In the last 20 years, I have traveled in nearly every continent and country—from Leningrad to Saigon, from Bucharest to Lima. From all of this, I have developed an image of America as fulfilling a noble and historic role as the defender of freedom in a time of maximum peril—and of the American people as confident, courageous and persevering.

It is with this image that I begin this campaign.

John F. Kennedy, speech to announce candidacy for president, January 2, 1960.

Document 2: Inaugural Address

Kennedy's inaugural address captured the spirit of his presidency and alluded to the policies he hoped to implement.

We observe today not a victory of party but a celebration of freedom, symbolizing an end as well as a beginning, signifying renewal as well as change. For I have sworn before you and Almighty God the same solemn oath our forebears prescribed nearly a century and three-quarters ago.

The world is very different now. For man holds in his mortal hands the power to abolish all forms of human poverty and all forms of human life. And yet the same revolutionary belief for which our forebears fought is still at issue around the globe, the belief that the rights of man come not from the generosity of the state but from the hand of God.

We dare not forget today that we are the heirs of that first revolution. Let the word go forth from this time and place, to friend and foe alike, that the torch has been passed to a new generation of Americans, born in this century, tempered by war, disciplined by a hard and bitter peace, proud of our ancient heritage, and unwilling to witness or permit the slow undoing of those human rights to which this nation has always been committed, and to which we are committed today at home and around the world.

Let every nation know, whether it wishes us well or ill, that we shall pay any price, bear any burden, meet any hardship, support any friend, oppose any foe to assure the survival and the success of liberty.

This much we pledge—and more.

To those old allies whose cultural and spiritual origins we share, we pledge the loyalty of faithful friends. United, there is little we cannot do in a host of co-operative ventures. Divided, there is little we can do, for we dare not meet a powerful challenge at odds and split asunder.

To those new states whom we welcome to the ranks of the free, we pledge our word that one form of colonial control shall not have passed away merely to be replaced by a far more iron tyranny. We shall not always expect to find them supporting our view. But we shall always hope to find them strongly supporting their own freedom, and to remember that, in the past, those who foolishly sought power by riding the back of the tiger ended up inside.

To those peoples in the huts and villages of half the globe struggling to break the bonds of mass misery, we pledge our best efforts to help them help themselves, for whatever period is required, not because the Communists may be doing it, not because we seek their votes, but because it is right. If a free society cannot help the many who are poor, it cannot save the few who are rich.

To our sister republics south of our border, we offer a special pledge: to convert our good words into good deeds, in a new alliance for progress, to assist free men and free governments in casting off the chains of poverty. But this peaceful revolution of hope cannot become the prey of hostile powers. Let all our neighbors know that we shall join with them to oppose agression or subversion anywhere in the Americas. And let every other power know that this hemisphere intends to remain the master of its own house.

To that world assembly of sovereign states, the United Nations, our last best hope in an age where the instruments of war have far outpaced the instruments of peace, we renew our pledge of support, to prevent it from becoming merely a forum for invective, to strengthen its shield of the new and the weak, and to enlarge the area in which its writ may run.

Finally, to those nations who would make themselves our adversary, we offer not a pledge but a request: that both sides begin anew the quest for peace, before the dark powers of destruction unleashed by science engulf all humanity in planned or accidental self-destruction.

We dare not tempt them with weakness. For only when our arms are sufficient beyond doubt can we be certain beyond doubt that they will never be employed.

But neither can two great and powerful groups of nations take comfort from our present course—both sides overburdened by the cost of modern weapons, both rightly alarmed by the steady spread of the deadly atom, yet both racing to alter that uncertain balance of terror that stays the hand of mankind's final war.

So let us begin anew, remembering on both sides that civility is not a sign of weakness, and sincerity is always subject to proof. Let us never negotiate out of fear, but let us never fear to negotiate.

Let both sides explore what problems unite us instead of belaboring those problems which divide us.

Let both sides, for the first time, formulate serious and precise proposals for the inspection and control of arms, and bring the absolute power to destroy other nations under the absolute control of all nations.

Let both sides seek to invoke the wonders of science instead of its terrors. Together let us explore the stars, conquer the deserts, eradicate disease, tap the ocean depths and encourage the arts and commerce.

Let both sides unite to heed in all corners of the earth the command of Isaiah to "undo the heavy burdens . . . [and] let the oppressed go free."

And if a beachhead of co-operation may push back the jungle of suspicion, let both sides join in creating a new endeavor, not a new balance of power, but a new world of law, where the strong are just and the weak secure and the peace preserved.

All this will not be finished in the first one hundred days. Nor will it be finished in the first one thousand days, nor in the life of this Administration, nor even perhaps in our lifetime on this planet. But let us begin.

In your hands, my fellow citizens, more than mine, will rest the final success or failure of our course. Since this country was founded, each generation of Americans has been summoned to give testimony to its national loyalty. The graves of young Americans who answered the call to service surround the globe.

Now the trumpet summons us again—not as a call to bear arms, though arms we need; not as a call to battle, though embattled we are; but a call to bear the burden of a long twilight struggle, year in and year out, "rejoicing in hope, patient in tribulation," a struggle against the common enemies of man: tyranny, poverty, disease and war itself.

Can we forge against these enemies a grand and global alliance, North and South, East and West, that can assure a more fruitful life for all mankind? Will you join in that historic effort?

In the long history of the world, only a few generations have been granted the role of defending freedom in its hour of maximum danger. I do not shrink from this responsibility; I welcome it. I do not believe that any of us would exchange places with any other people or any other generation. The energy, the faith, the devotion which we bring to this endeavor will light our country and all who serve it, and the glow from that fire can truly light the world.

And so, my fellow Americans, ask not what your country can do for you; ask what you can do for your country.

My fellow citizens of the world, ask not what America will do for you, but what together we can do for the freedom of man.

Finally, whether you are citizens of America or citizens of the world, ask of us here the same high standards of strength and sacrifice which we ask of you. With a good conscience our only sure reward, with history the final judge of our deeds, let us go forth to lead the land we love, asking His blessing and His help, but knowing that here on earth God's work must truly be our own.

John F. Kennedy, inaugural address, January 20, 1961.

Document 3: Special Message to Congress on the Peace Corps

One of Kennedy's most popular and enduring legacies is the Peace Corps. Here Kennedy details for Congress his plans to establish a youth volunteer program to station young Americans in developing countries to provide aid for indigenous populations.

I recommend to the Congress the establishment of a permanent Peace Corps, *a pool of trained American men and women sent overseas by the U.S. Government or through private organizations and institutions to help foreign countries meet their urgent needs for skilled manpower.* . . .

Throughout the world the people of the newly developing nations are struggling for economic and social progress which reflects their deepest desires. Our own freedom, and the future of freedom around the world, depend . . . on their ability to build growing and independent nations where men can live in dignity, liberated from the bonds of hunger, ignorance and poverty.

One of the greatest obstacles to the achievement of this goal is the lack of trained men and women with the skill to teach the young and assist in the operation of development projects, men and women with the capacity to cope with the demands of swiftly evolving economies, and with the dedication to put that capacity to work in the villages, the mountains, the towns and the factories of dozens of struggling nations.

The vast task of economic development urgently requires skilled people to do the work of the society: to help teach in the schools, construct development projects, demonstrate modern methods of sanitation in the villages, and perform a hundred other tasks calling for training and advanced knowledge.

To meet this urgent need for skilled manpower we are proposing the establishment of a Peace Corps, an organization which will recruit and train American volunteers, sending them abroad to work with the people of other nations.

This organization will differ from existing assistance programs in that its members will supplement technical advisers by offering the specific skills needed by developing nations if they are to put technical advice to work. They will help provide the skilled manpower necessary to carry out the development projects planned by the host governments, acting at a working level and serving at great personal sacrifice. There is little doubt that the number of those who wish to serve will be far greater than our capacity to absorb them. . . .

Most heartening of all, the initial reaction to this proposal has been an enthusiastic response by student groups, professional organizations and private citizens everywhere, a convincing demonstration that we have in this country an immense reservoir of dedicated men and women willing to devote their energies and time and toil to the cause of world peace and human progress.

Among the specific programs to which Peace Corps members can contribute are: teaching in primary and secondary schools, especially as part of national English-language-teaching programs; participation in the world-wide program of malaria eradication; instruction and operation of public health and sanitation projects; aiding in village development through school construction and other programs; increasing rural agricultural productivity by assisting local farmers to use modern implements and techniques. The initial emphasis of these programs will be on teaching. . . .

The Peace Corps will not be limited to the young, or to college graduates. All Americans who are qualified will be welcome to join this effort. But undoubtedly the Corps will be made up primarily of young people as they complete their formal education.

Because one of the greatest resources of a free society is the strength and diversity of its private organizations and institutions, much of the Peace Corps program will be carried out by these groups, financially assisted by the Federal Government.

Peace Corps personnel will be made available to developing nations in the following ways:

1. Through private voluntary agencies carrying on international assistance programs.
2. Through overseas programs of colleges and universities.
3. Through assistance programs of international agencies.
4. Through assistance programs of the United States Government.

5. Through new programs which the Peace Corps itself directly administers. . . .

In all instances the men and women of the Peace Corps will go only to those countries where their services and skills are genuinely needed and desired. . . .

Length of service in the Corps will vary depending on the kind of project and the country, generally ranging from two to three years. Peace Corps members will often serve under conditions of physical hardship, living under primitive conditions among the people of developing nations. For every Peace Corps member service will mean a great financial sacrifice. They will receive no salary. Instead they will be given an allowance which will only be sufficient to meet their basic needs and maintain health. It is essential that Peace Corpsmen and women live simply and unostentatiously among the people they have come to assist. At the conclusion of their tours, members of the Peace Corps will receive a small sum in the form of severance pay based on length of service abroad, to assist them during their first weeks back in the United States. Service with the Peace Corps will not exempt volunteers from Selective Service. . . .

Although this is an American Peace Corps, the problem of world development is not just an American problem. Let us hope that other nations will mobilize the spirit and energies and skill of their people in some form of Peace Corps, making our own effort only one step in a major international effort to increase the welfare of all men and improve understanding among nations.

John F. Kennedy, special message to Congress on the Peace Corps, March 1, 1961.

Document 4: Speech on the Alliance for Progress Diplomats

Relations between the United States and Latin America had deteriorated significantly during the Eisenhower administration. Kennedy sought to improve relations through increased aid and programs such as the Alliance for Progress.

For the first time we have the capacity to strike off the remaining bonds of poverty and ignorance, to free our people for the spiritual and intellectual fulfillment which has always been the goal of our civilization.

Yet at this very moment of maximum opportunity, we confront the same forces which have imperiled America throughout its history, the alien forces which once again seek to impose the despotisms of the old world on the people of the new. . . .

Our . . . task is to demonstrate to the entire world that man's unsatisfied aspiration for economic progress and social justice can best be achieved by free men working within a framework of democratic institutions. If we can do this in our own hemisphere, and for our own people, we may yet realize the prophecy of the great Mexican patriot, Benito Juárez, that "democracy is the destiny of future humanity.". . .

Therefore I have called on all the people of the hemisphere to join in a new Alliance for Progress—*Alianza para Progreso*—vast cooperative effort, unparalleled in magnitude and nobility of purpose, to satisfy the basic needs of the American people for homes, work and land, health and schools—*techo, trabajo y tierra, salud y escuela.*

First, I propose that the American Republics begin on a vast new Ten-Year Plan for the Americas, a plan to transform the 1960's into an historic decade of democratic progress.

These ten years will be the years of maximum progress, maximum effort, the years when the greatest obstacles must be overcome, the years when the need for assistance will be the greatest. . . .

If the countries of Latin America are ready to do their part, and I am sure they are, then I believe the United States, for its part, should help provide resources of a scope and magnitude sufficient to make this bold development plan a success, just as we helped to provide, against equal odds nearly, the resources adequate to help rebuild the economies of Western Europe. For only an effort of towering dimensions can ensure fulfillment of our plan for a decade of progress.

Second, I will shortly request a ministerial meeting of the Inter-American Economic and Social Council, a meeting at which we can begin the massive planning effort which will be at the heart of the Alliance for Progress.

For if our Alliance is to succeed, each Latin nation must formulate long-range plans for its own development, plans which establish targets and priorities, ensure monetary stability, establish the machinery for vital social change, stimulate private activity and initiative, and provide for a maximum national effort. These plans will be the foundation of our development effort, and the basis for the allocation of outside resources. . . .

Third, I have this evening signed a request to the Congress for $500 million as a first step in fulfilling the Act of Bogotá. This is the first large-scale inter-American effort, instituted by my predecessor President Eisenhower, to attack the social barriers which block economic progress. The money will be used to combat illiteracy, improve the productivity and use of the land, wipe out disease, attack archaic tax and land tenure structures, provide educational opportunities and offer a broad range of projects designed to make the benefits of increasing abundance available to all. . . .

Fourth, we must support all economic integration which is a genuine step toward larger markets and greater competitive opportunity. The fragmentation of Latin-American economies is a serious barrier to industrial growth. Projects such as the Central American common market and free trade areas in South America can help to remove these obstacles.

Fifth, the United States is ready to co-operate in serious, case-by-case examinations of commodity market problems. Frequent violent changes in commodity prices seriously injure the economies of many Latin-American countries, draining their resources, and stultifying their growth. . . .

Sixth, we will immediately step up our Food-for-Peace emergency program, help to establish food reserves in areas of recurrent drought, and help provide school lunches for children and offer feed grains for use in rural development. . . .

Seventh, all the people of the hemisphere must be allowed to share in the expanding wonders of science, wonders which have captured man's imagination, challenged the powers of his mind, and given him the tools for rapid progress. I invite Latin-American scientists to work with us in new projects in fields such as medicine and agriculture, physics and astronomy and desalinization; and to help plan for regional research laboratories in these and other fields; and to strengthen co-operation between American universities and laboratories.

We also intend to expand our science-teacher-training programs to include Latin-American instructors, to assist in establishing such programs in other American countries, and translate and make available revolutionary new teaching materials in physics, chemistry, biology and mathematics, so that the young of all nations may contribute their skills to the advance of science.

Eighth, we must rapidly expand the training of those needed to man the economies of rapidly developing countries. This means expanded technical training programs, for which the Peace Corps, for example, will be available when needed. It also means assistance to Latin-American universities, graduate schools and research institutes. . . .

Ninth, we reaffirm our pledge to come to the defense of any American nation whose independence is endangered. As its confidence in the collective security system of the Organization of American States spreads, it will be possible to devote to constructive use a major share of those resources now spent on the instruments of war. Even now, as the government of Chile has said, the time has come to take the first steps toward sensible limitations of arms. And the new generation of military leaders has shown an increasing awareness that armies cannot only defend their countries; they can, as we have learned through our own Corps of Engineers, help to build them.

Tenth, we invite our friends in Latin America to contribute to the enrichment of life and culture in the United States. We need teachers of your literature and history and tradition, opportunities for our young people to study in your universities, access to your music, your art and the thought of your great philosophers. For we know we have much to learn. . . .

With steps such as these, we propose to complete the revolution of the Americas, to build a hemisphere where all men can hope for a suitable standard of living, and all can live out their lives in dignity and in freedom.

To achieve this goal political freedom must accompany material progress. Our Alliance for Progress is an alliance of free governments, and it must work to eliminate tyranny from a hemisphere in which it has no rightful place. Therefore let us express our special friendship to the people of Cuba and the Dominican Republic, and the hope they will soon rejoin the society of free men, uniting with us in our common effort.

This political freedom must be accompanied by social change. For unless necessary social reforms, including land and tax reform, are freely made; unless we broaden the opportunity of all of our people; unless the great mass of Americans share in increasing prosperity, then our alliance, our revolution, our dream and our freedom will fail. But we call for social change by free men, change in the spirit of Washington and Jefferson, of Bolívar and San Martín and Martí, not change which seeks to impose on men tyrannies which we cast out a century and a half ago. Our motto is what it has always been: "Progress yes, tyranny no—*Progreso sí, tiranía no!*"

John F. Kennedy, address at a reception for Latin American diplomats, March 13, 1961.

Document 5: Special Message to Congress on Foreign Aid

Early during his presidency, Kennedy presented the framework for aid policy that he hoped to develop. The young president called for a dramatic reorientation of U.S. aid policy so that American assistance would be based on need and results, not just strategic considerations.

This nation must begin any discussion of "foreign aid" in 1961 with the recognition of three facts:

1. Existing foreign aid programs and concepts are largely unsatisfactory and unsuited for our needs and for the needs of the underdeveloped world as it enters the sixties.

2. The economic collapse of those free but less developed nations which now stand poised between sustained growth and economic chaos would be disastrous to our national security, harmful to our comparative prosperity and offensive to our conscience.

3. There exists, in the 1960's, an historic opportunity for a major economic assistance effort by the free industrialized nations to move more than half the people of the less-developed nations into self-sustained economic growth, while the rest move substantially closer to the day when they, too, will no longer have to depend on outside assistance.

Foreign aid, America's unprecedented response to world challenge, has not been the work of one party or one Administration. It has moved forward under the leadership of two great Presidents, Harry Truman and Dwight Eisenhower, and drawn its support from forward-looking members of both political parties in the Congress and throughout the nation.

Our first major foreign aid effort was an emergency program of relief, of food and clothing and shelter, to areas devastated by World War II. Next we embarked on the Marshall Plan, a towering and successful program to rebuild the economies of Western Europe and prevent a Communist takeover. This was followed by Point Four, an effort to make scientific and technological advances available to the people of developing nations. And recently the concept of development assistance, coupled with the Organization for Economic Co-operation and Development, has opened the door to a united free world effort to assist the economic and social development of the less-developed areas of the world.

To achieve this new goal we will need to renew the spirit of common effort which lay behind our past efforts. We must also revise our foreign aid organization, and our basic concepts of operation to meet the new problems which now confront us.

For no objective supporter of foreign aid can be satisfied with the existing program, actually a multiplicity of programs. Bureaucratically fragmented, awkward and slow, its administration is diffused over a haphazard and irrational structure covering at least four departments and several other agencies. The program is based on a series of legislative measures and administrative procedures conceived at different times and for different purposes, many of them now obsolete, inconsistent and unduly rigid and thus unsuited for our present needs and purposes. Its weaknesses have begun to undermine confidence in our effort both here and abroad. . . .

We live at a very special moment in history. . . . Latin America, Africa, the Middle East and Asia are caught up in the adventures of asserting their independence and modernizing their old ways of life. These new nations need aid in loans and technical assistance just as we in the northern half of the world drew successively on one another's capital and know-how as we moved into industrialization and regular growth.

But in our time these new nations need help for a special reason. Without exception they are under Communist pressure. In many cases, that pressure is direct and military. In others, it takes the form of intense subversive activity designed to break down and supersede the new, and often frail, modern institutions they have thus far built.

But the fundamental task of our foreign aid program in the 1960's is not negatively to fight Communism. Its fundamental task is to help make an historical demonstration that in the twentieth century as in the nineteenth, in the southern half of the globe as in the north, economic growth and political democracy can develop hand in hand.

In short, we have not only obligations to fulfill; we have great opportunities to realize. We are, I am convinced, on the threshold of a truly united and major effort by the free industrialized nations to assist the less-developed nations on a long-term basis. Many of these less-developed nations are on the threshold of achieving sufficient economic, social and political strength and self-sustained growth to stand permanently on their own feet. The 1960's can be, and must be, the crucial "Decade of Development"; the period when many less-developed nations make the transition into self-sustained growth; the period in which an enlarged community of free, stable and self-reliant nations can reduce world tensions and insecurity. *This goal is in our grasp if, and only if, the other industrialized nations now join us in developing with the recipients a set of commonly agreed criteria, a set of long-range goals, and a common undertaking to meet those goals, in which each nation's contribution is related to the contributions of others and to the precise needs of each less-developed nation.* Our job, in its largest sense, is to create a new partnership between the northern and southern halves of the world, to which all free nations can contribute, in which each free nation must assume a responsibility proportional to its means. . . .

In short, this Congress at this session must make possible a dramatic turning point in the troubled history of foreign aid to the underde-veloped world. We must say to the less-developed nations, *if they are willing to undertake necessary internal reform and self-help*, and to the other industrialized nations, *if they are willing to undertake a much greater effort on a much broader scale*, that we then intend during this coming decade of development to achieve a decisive turn-around in the fate of the less-developed world, looking toward the ultimate day when all nations can be self-reliant and when foreign aid will no longer be needed. . . .

This will require leadership, by this country in this year. And it will require a fresh approach, a more logical, efficient and successful long-term plan, for American foreign aid. I strongly recommend to the Congress the enactment of such a plan, as contained in a measure to be sent shortly to the Congress and described below.

If our foreign aid funds are to be prudently and effectively used, we need a whole new set of basic concepts and principles:

1. Unified administration and operation—a single agency in Washington and the field, equipped with a flexible set of tools, in place of several competing and confusing aid units.

2. Country plans—a carefully thought-through program tailored to meet the needs and the resource potential of each individual country, instead of a series of individual, unrelated projects. Frequently, in the past, our development goals and projects have not been undertaken as integral steps in a long-range economic development program.

3. Long-term planning and financing, the only way to make meaningful and economical commitments.

4. Special emphasis on development loans repayable in dollars, more conducive to business-like relations and mutual respect than sustaining grants or loans repaid in local currencies, although some instances of the latter are unavoidable.

5. Special attention to those nations most willing and able to mobilize their own resources, make necessary social and economic reforms, engage in long-range planning, and make the other efforts necessary if these are to reach the stage of self-sustaining growth.

6. Multilateral approach—a program and level of commitments designed to encourage and complement an increased effort by other industrialized nations.

7. A new agency with new personnel, drawing upon the most competent and dedicated career servants now in the field, and attracting the highest quality from every part of the nation.

8. Separation from military assistance. Our program of aid to social

and economic development must be seen on its own merits, and judged in the light of its vital and distinctive contribution to our basic security needs. . . .

I recommend, therefore, an authorization for the new aid agency of not less than five years, with borrowing authority also for five years to commit and make dollar repayable loans within the limits spelled out below. No other step would be such a clear signal of our intentions to all the world. No other step would do more to help obtain the service of top-flight personnel. And in no other way can we encourage the less-developed nations to make a sustained national effort over a long-term period.

For, if we are to have a program designed to brighten the future, that program must have a future. . . .

John F. Kennedy, special message to Congress on foreign aid, March 22, 1961.

Document 6: The President and the Press

In his April 27, 1961, address to the American Newspaper Publishers Association in New York City, Kennedy shared his thoughts on the relationship between the president and the press.

I have selected as the title of my remarks tonight "The President and the Press." Some may suggest that this would be more naturally worded "The President Versus the Press." But those are not my sentiments tonight. . . .

I want to talk about our common responsibilities in the face of a common danger. The events of recent weeks may have helped to illuminate that challenge for some; but the dimensions of its threat have loomed large on the horizon for many years. Whatever our hopes may be for the future—for reducing this threat or living with it—there is no escaping either the gravity or the totality of its challenge to our survival and to our security—a challenge that confronts us in unaccustomed ways in every sphere of human activity.

This deadly challenge imposes upon our society two requirements of direct concern both to the press and to the President—two requirements that may seem almost contradictory in tone, but which must be reconciled and fulfilled if we are to meet this national peril. I refer, first, to the need for a far greater public information; and, second, to the need for far greater official secrecy. . . .

For the facts of the matter are that this nation's foes have openly boasted of acquiring through our newspapers information they would otherwise hire agents to acquire through theft, bribery or espionage;

that details of this nation's covert preparations to counter the enemy's covert operations have been available to every newspaper reader, friend and foe alike; that the size, the strength, the location and the nature of our forces and weapons, and our plans and strategy for their use, have all been pinpointed in the press and other news media to a degree sufficient to satisfy any foreign power; and that, in at least in one case, the publication of details concerning a secret mechanism whereby satellites were followed required its alteration at the expense of considerable time and money.

The newspapers which printed these stories were loyal, patriotic, responsible and well-meaning. Had we been engaged in open warfare, they undoubtedly would not have published such items. But in the absence of open warfare, they recognized only the tests of journalism and not the tests of national security. And my question tonight is whether additional tests should not now be adopted.

The question is for you alone to answer. No public official should answer it for you. No governmental plan should impose its restraints against your will. But I would be failing in my duty to the nation, in considering all of the responsibilities that we now bear and all of the means at hand to meet those responsibilities, if I did not commend this problem to your attention, and urge its thoughtful consideration.

On many earlier occasions, I have said—and your newspapers have constantly said—that these are times that appeal to every citizen's sense of sacrifice and self-discipline. They call out to every citizen to weigh his rights and comforts against his obligations to the common good. I cannot now believe that those citizens who serve in the newspaper business consider themselves exempt from that appeal.

I have no intention of establishing a new Office of War Information to govern the flow of news. I am not suggesting any new forms of censorship or any new types of security classifications. I have no easy answer to the dilemma that I have posed, and would not seek to impose it if I had one. But I am asking the members of the newspaper profession and the industry in this country to reexamine their own responsibilities, to consider the degree and the nature of the present danger, and to heed the duty of self-restraint which that danger imposes upon us all. . . .

It is the unprecedented nature of this challenge that also gives rise to your second obligation—an obligation which I share. And that is our obligation to inform and alert the American people—to make certain that they possess all the facts that they need, and understand them as well—the perils, the prospects, the purposes of our program and the choices that we face.

No President should fear public scrutiny of his program. For from that scrutiny comes understanding; and from that understanding comes support or opposition. And both are necessary. I am not asking your newspapers to support the Administration, but I am asking your help in the tremendous task of informing and alerting the American people. For I have complete confidence in the response and dedication of our citizens whenever they are fully informed.

I not only could not stifle controversy among your readers—I welcome it. This Administration intends to be candid about its errors; for as a wise man once said: "An error does not become a mistake until you refuse to correct it." We intend to accept full responsibility for our errors; and we expect you to point them out when we miss them.

Without debate, without criticism, no Administration and no country can succeed—and no republic can survive. That is why the Athenian lawmaker Solon decreed it a crime for any citizen to shrink from controversy. And that is why our press was protected by the First Amendment—the only business in America specifically protected by the Constitution—not primarily to amuse and entertain, not to emphasize the trivial and the sentimental, not to simply "give the public what it wants"—but to inform, to arouse, to reflect, to state our dangers and our opportunities, to indicate our crises and our choices, to lead, mold, educate and sometimes even anger public opinion.

This means greater coverage and analysis of international news—for it is no longer far away and foreign but close at hand and local. It means greater attention to improved understanding of the news as well as improved transmission. And it means, finally, that government at all levels, must meet its obligation to provide you with the fullest possible information outside the narrowest limits of national security—and we intend to do it.

John F. Kennedy, address to the American Newspaper Publishers Association, New York City, April 27, 1961.

Document 7: Report to the Nation on the Berlin Crisis

The Berlin crisis was an early foreign policy test for Kennedy. The actions of the Soviet Union reinforced Kennedy's perception of the need to improve American military capabilities. In his address to the American people, Kennedy calls upon the nation to support increases in military spending.

Seven weeks ago tonight I returned from Europe to report on my meeting with Premier Khrushchev and the others. His grim warnings about the future of the world, his *aide-mémoire* on Berlin, his subsequent speeches and threats which he and his agents have launched, and the increase in the Soviet military budget that he has announced, have all prompted a series of decisions by the Administration and a series of consultations with the members of the North Atlantic Treaty Organization. In Berlin, as you recall, he intends to bring to an end, through a stroke of the pen, first, our legal rights to be in West Berlin and, second, our ability to make good on our commitment to the two million free people of that city. That we cannot permit.

We are clear about what must be done, and we intend to do it. I want to talk frankly with you tonight about the first steps that we shall take. These actions will require sacrifice on the part of many of our citizens. More will be required in the future. They will require, from all of us, courage and perseverance in the years to come. But if we and our allies act out of strength and unity of purpose, with calm determination and steady nerves, using restraint in our words as well as our weapons, I am hopeful that both peace and freedom will be sustained.

The immediate threat to free men is in West Berlin. But that isolated outpost is not an isolated problem. The threat is worldwide. Our effort must be equally wide and strong, and not be obsessed by any single manufactured crisis. We face a challenge in Berlin, but there is also a challenge in Southeast Asia, where the borders are less guarded, the enemy harder to find, and the danger of Communism less apparent to those who have so little. We face a challenge in our own hemisphere, and indeed wherever else the freedom of human beings is at stake.

Let me remind you that the fortunes of war and diplomacy left the free people of West Berlin in 1945 110 miles behind the Iron Curtain....

It would be a mistake for others to look upon Berlin, because of its location, as a tempting target. The United States is there; the United Kingdom and France are there; the pledge of NATO is there; and the people of Berlin are there. It is as secure, in that sense, as the rest of us, for we cannot separate its safety from our own.

I hear it said that West Berlin is militarily untenable. And so was Bastogne. And so, in fact, was Stalingrad. Any dangerous spot is tenable if men—brave men—will make it so.

We do not want to fight, but we have fought before. And others in earlier times have made the same dangerous mistake of assuming that the West was too selfish and too soft and too divided to resist invasions of freedom in other lands. Those who threaten to unleash the forces of war on a dispute over West Berlin should recall the words of the ancient philosopher: "A man who causes fear cannot be free from fear."

We cannot and will not permit the Communists to drive us out of

Berlin, either gradually or by force. For the fulfillment of our pledge to that city is essential to the morale and security of Western Germany, to the unity of Western Europe, and to the faith of the entire free world. Soviet strategy has long been aimed, not merely at Berlin, but at dividing and neutralizing all of Europe, forcing us back to our own shores. We must meet our oft-stated pledge to the free peoples of West Berlin, and maintain our rights and their safety, even in the face of force, in order to maintain the confidence of other free peoples in our word and our resolve. The strength of the alliance on which our security depends is dependent in turn on our willingness to meet our commitments to them.

So long as the Communists insist that they are preparing to end by themselves unilaterally our rights in West Berlin and our commitments to its people, we must be prepared to defend those rights and those commitments. We will at all times be ready to talk, if talk will help. But we must also be ready to resist with force, if force is used upon us. Either alone would fail. Together, they can serve the cause of freedom and peace. . . .

As signers on the United Nations Charter, we shall always be prepared to discuss international problems with any and all nations that are willing to talk, and listen, with reason. If they have proposals, not demands, we shall hear them. If they seek genuine understanding, not concessions of our rights, we shall meet with them. We have previously indicated our readiness to remove any actual irritants in West Berlin, but the freedom of that city is not negotiable. We cannot negotiate with those who say, "What's mine is mine and what's yours is negotiable." But we are willing to consider any arrangement or treaty in Germany consistent with the maintenance of peace and freedom, and with the legitimate security interests of all nations.

We recognize the Soviet Union's historical concerns about their security in Central and Eastern Europe, after a series of ravaging invasions, and we believe arrangements can be worked out which will help to meet those concerns, and make it possible for both security and freedom to exist in this troubled area.

For it is not the freedom of West Berlin which is "abnormal" in Germany today, but the situation in that entire divided country. If anyone doubts the legality of our rights in Berlin, we are ready to have it submitted to international adjudication. If anyone doubts the extent to which our presence is desired by the people of West Berlin, compared to East German feelings about their regime, we are ready to have that question submitted to a free vote in Berlin and, if possible, among all the German people. And let us hear at that time from the two and one-half million refugees who have fled the Communist regime in East Germany, voting for Western-type freedom with their feet.

The world is not deceived by the Communist attempt to label Berlin as a hotbed of war. There is peace in Berlin today. The source of world trouble and tension is Moscow, not Berlin. And if war begins, it will have begun in Moscow and not Berlin.

For the choice of peace or war is largely theirs, not ours. It is the Soviets who have stirred up this crisis. It is they who are trying to force a change. It is they who have opposed free elections. It is they who have rejected an all-German peace treaty, and the rulings of international law. And as Americans know from our history on our own old frontier, gun battles are caused by outlaws, and not by officers of the peace. . . .

We in the West must move together in building military strength. We must consult one another more closely than ever before. We must together design our proposals for peace, and labor together as they are pressed at the conference table. And together we must share the burdens and the risks of this effort.

The Atlantic Community, as we know it, has been built in response to challenge: the challenge of European chaos in 1947; of the Berlin blockade in 1948, the challenge of Communist aggression in Korea in 1950. Now, standing strong and prosperous, after an unprecedented decade of progress, the Atlantic Community will not forget either its history or the principles which gave it meaning.

The solemn vow each of us gave to West Berlin in time of peace will not be broken in time of danger. If we do not meet our commitments to Berlin, where will we later stand? If we are not true to our word there, all that we have achieved in collective security, which relies on these words, will mean nothing. And if there is one path above all others to war, it is the path of weakness and disunity.

Today, the endangered frontier of freedom runs through divided Berlin. We want it to remain a frontier of peace. This is the hope of every citizen of the Atlantic Community; every citizen of Eastern Europe; and, I am confident, every citizen of the Soviet Union. For I cannot believe that the Russian people, who bravely suffered enormous losses in the Second World War, would now wish to see the peace upset once more in Germany. The Soviet Government alone can convert Berlin's frontier of peace into a pretext for war.

The steps I have indicated tonight are aimed at avoiding that war. To sum it all up: we seek peace, but we shall not surrender. That is the central meaning of this crisis, and the meaning of your government's policy.

With your help, and the help of other free men, this crisis can be surmounted. Freedom can prevail, and peace can endure.

John F. Kennedy, report to the nation on the Berlin crisis, July 25, 1961.

Document 8: Desegregating the University of Mississippi

On September 30, 1962, Kennedy delivered a national television and radio address on the tense situation at the University of Mississippi involving the attempted enrollment of a black student.

Good evening my fellow citizens:

The orders of the court in the case of Meredith versus Fair are beginning to be carried out. Mr. James Meredith is now in residence on the campus of the University of Mississippi.

This has been accomplished thus far without the use of National Guard or other troops. And it is to be hoped that the law enforcement officers of the State of Mississippi and the Federal marshals will continue to be sufficient in the future.

All students, members of the faculty, and public officials in both Mississippi and the Nation will be able, it is hoped, to return to their normal activities with full confidence in the integrity of American law.

This is as it should be, for our Nation is founded on the principle that observance of the law is the eternal safeguard of liberty and defiance of the law is the surest road to tyranny. The law which we obey includes the final rulings of the courts, as well as the enactments of our legislative bodies. Even among law-abiding men few laws are universally loved, but they are uniformly respected and not resisted.

Americans are free, in short, to disagree with the law but not to disobey it. For in a government of laws and not of men, no man, however prominent or powerful, and no mob however unruly or boisterous, is entitled to defy a court of law. If this country should ever reach the point where any man or group of men by force or threat of force could long defy the commands of our court and our Constitution, then no law would stand free from doubt, no judge would be sure of his writ, and no citizen would be safe from his neighbors.

In this case in which the United States Government was not until recently involved, Mr. Meredith brought a private suit in Federal court against those who were excluding him from the University. A series of Federal courts all the way to the Supreme Court repeatedly ordered Mr. Meredith's admission to the University. When those orders were defied, and those who sought to implement them were threatened with arrest and violence, the United States Court of Appeals consisting of Chief

Judge Tuttle of Georgia, Judge Hutcheson of Texas, Judge Rives of Alabama, Judge Jones of Florida, Judge Brown of Texas, Judge Wisdom of Louisiana, Judge Gewin of Alabama, and Judge Bell of Georgia, made clear the fact that the enforcement of its order had become an obligation of the United States Government. Even though this Government had not originally been a party to the case, my responsibility as President was therefore inescapable. I accept it. My obligation under the Constitution and the statutes of the United States was and is to implement the orders of the court with whatever means are necessary, and with as little force and civil disorder as the circumstances permit.

It was for this reason that I federalized the Mississippi National Guard as the most appropriate instrument, should any be needed, to preserve law and order while United States marshals carried out the orders of the court and prepared to back them up with whatever other civil or military enforcement might have been required.

I deeply regret the fact that any action by the executive branch was necessary in this case, but all other avenues and alternatives, including persuasion and conciliation, had been tried and exhausted. Had the police powers of Mississippi been used to support the orders of the court, instead of deliberately and unlawfully blocking them, had the University of Mississippi fulfilled its standard of excellence by quietly admitting this applicant in conformity with what so many other southern State universities have done for so many years, a peaceable and sensible solution would have been possible without any Federal intervention.

This Nation is proud of the many instances in which Governors, educators, and everyday citizens from the South have shown to the world the gains that can be made by persuasion and good will in a society ruled by law. Specifically, I would like to take this occasion to express the thanks of this Nation to those southerners who have contributed to the progress of our democratic development in the entrance of students regardless of race to such great institutions as the State-supported universities of Virginia, North Carolina, Georgia, Florida, Texas, Louisiana, Tennessee, Arkansas, and Kentucky.

I recognize that the present period of transition and adjustment in our Nation's Southland is a hard one for many people. Neither Mississippi nor any other southern State deserves to be charged with all the accumulated wrongs of the last 100 years of race relations. To the extent that there has been failure, the responsibility for that failure must be shared by us all, by every State, by every citizen.

Mississippi and her University, moreover, are noted for their courage, for their contribution of talent and thought to the affairs of this Nation. This is the State of Lucius Lamar and many others who have placed the national good ahead of sectional interest. This is the State which had four Medal of Honor winners in the Korean War alone. In fact, the Guard unit federalized this morning, early, is part of the 155th Infantry, one of the 10 oldest regiments in the Union and one of the most decorated for sacrifice and bravery in 6 wars.

In 1945 a Mississippi sergeant, Jake Lindsey, was honored by an unusual joint session of the Congress. I close therefore, with this appeal to the students of the University, the people who are most concerned.

You have a great tradition to uphold, a tradition of honor and courage won on the field of battle and on the gridiron as well as the University campus. You have a new opportunity to show that you are men of patriotism and integrity. For the most effective means of upholding the law is not the State policeman or the marshals or the National Guard. It is you. It lies in your courage to accept those laws with which you disagree as well as those with which you agree. The eyes of the Nation and of all the world are upon you and upon all of us, and the honor of your University and State are in the balance. I am certain that the great majority of the students will uphold that honor.

There is in short no reason why the books on this case cannot now be quickly and quietly closed in the manner directed by the court. Let us preserve both the law and the peace and then healing those wounds that are within we can turn to the greater crises that are without and stand united as one people in our pledge to man's freedom.

Thank you and good night.

John F. Kennedy, address to the nation, September 30, 1962.

Document 9: Address to the American People on the Cuban Missile Crisis

The American public listened anxiously to Kennedy's address on the status of the Cuban missile crisis, delivered on October 22, 1962, amid concern about nuclear war with the Soviet Union.

This Government, as promised, has maintained the closest surveillance of the Soviet military buildup on the island of Cuba. Within the past week, unmistakable evidence has established the fact that a series of offensive missile sites is now in preparation on that imprisoned island. The purpose of these bases can be none other than to provide a nuclear strike capability against the Western hemisphere.

Upon receiving the first preliminary hard information of this nature last Tuesday morning at 9 A.M., I directed that our surveillance be stepped up. And having now confirmed and completed our evaluation of the evidence and our decision on a course of action, this Government feels obliged to report this new crisis to you in full detail.

The characteristics of these new missile sites indicate two distinct types of installations. Several of them include medium-range ballistic missiles, capable of carrying a nuclear warhead for a distance of more than 1,000 nautical miles. Each of these missiles, in short, is capable of striking Washington, D.C., the Panama Canal, Cape Canaveral, Mexico City, or any other city in the Eastern part of the United States, in Central America or in the Caribbean area.

Additional sites not yet completed appear to be designed for intermediate-range ballistic missiles—capable of travelling more than twice as far—and thus capable of striking most of the major cities in the Western hemisphere, ranging as far North as Hudson's Bay, Canada, and as far South as Lima, Peru. In addition, jet bombers, capable of carrying nuclear weapons, are now being uncrated and assembled on Cuba, while the necessary air bases are being prepared.

This urgent transformation of Cuba into an important strategic base—by the presence of these large, long-range and clearly offensive weapons of sudden mass destruction—constitutes an explicit threat to the peace and security of all the Americas, in flagrant and deliberate defiance of the Rio Pact of 1947, the traditions of this nation and hemisphere, the joint resolution of the 87th Congress, the Charter of the United Nations and my own public warnings to the Soviets on 4 and 13 September. This action also contradicts the repeated assurances of Soviet spokesmen, both publicly and privately delivered, that the arms buildup in Cuba would retain its original defensive character, and that the Soviet Union had no need or desire to station strategic missiles on the territory of any other nation. . . .

For many years, both the Soviet Union and the United States—recognizing this fact—have deployed strategic nuclear weapons with great care, never upsetting the precarious *status quo* which ensured that these weapons would not be used in the absence of some vital challenge. Our own strategic missiles have never been transferred to the territory of any other nation under a cloak of secrecy and deception; and our history—unlike that of the Soviets since World War II—demonstrates that we have no desire to dominate or conquer any other nation or impose our system upon its people.

Nevertheless, American citizens have become adjusted to living daily on the bull's-eye of Soviet missiles located inside the USSR or in submarines. In that sense, missiles in Cuba add to an already clear and present danger—although, it should be noted, the nations of Latin America have never previously been subjected to a potential nuclear threat.

But this secret, swift and extraordinary buildup of Communist missiles—in an area well-known to have a special and historical relationship to the United States and the nations of the Western hemisphere, in violation of Soviet assurances, and in defiance of American and hemispheric policy—this sudden decision to station strategic weapons for the first time outside of Soviet soil—is a deliberately provocative and unjustified change in the *status quo* which cannot be accepted by this country, if our courage and our commitments are ever to be trusted again by either friend or foe. . . .

Acting, therefore, in the defense of our own security and that of the entire Western hemisphere, and under the authority entrusted to me by the Constitution as endorsed by the resolution of the Congress, I have directed that the following initial steps be taken immediately:

First: to halt this offensive buildup, a strict quarantine on all offensive military equipment under shipment to Cuba is being initiated. All ships of any kind bound for Cuba, from whatever nation or port, will, if found to contain cargoes of offensive weapons, be turned back. This quarantine will be extended, if needed, to other types of cargo and carriers. We are not at this time, however, denying the necessities of life as the Soviets attempted to do in their Berlin blockade of 1948.

Second: I have directed the continued and increased close surveillance of Cuba and its military buildup. . . . I have directed the Armed Forces to prepare for any eventualities; and I trust that, in the interest of both the Cuban people and the Soviet technicians at these sites, the hazards to all concerned of continuing this threat will be recognized.

Third: It shall be the policy of this nation to regard any nuclear missile launched from Cuba against any nation in the Western hemisphere as an attack by the Soviet Union on the United States requiring a full retaliatory response upon the Soviet Union.

Fourth: As a necessary military precaution, I have reinforced our base at Guantanamo, evacuated today the dependents of our personnel there and ordered additional military units to be on a standby alert basis.

Fifth: We are calling tonight for an immediate meeting of the Organ of Consultation under the Organisation of American States, to consider this threat to hemispheric security and to invoke Articles 6 and 8 of the Rio Treaty in support of all necessary action. The United Nations Charter allows for regional security arrangements, and the nations of this hemisphere decided long ago against the military presence of outside powers. Our other Allies around the world have also been alerted.

Sixth: Under the Charter of the United Nations, we are asking tonight that an emergency meeting of the Security Council be convoked without delay to take action against this latest Soviet threat to world peace. Our resolution will call for the prompt dismantling and withdrawal of all offensive weapons in Cuba, under the supervision of U.N. observers, before the quarantine can be lifted.

Seventh, and finally: I call upon Chairman Khrushchev to halt and eliminate this clandestine, reckless and provocative threat to world peace and to stable relations between our two nations. I call upon him further to abandon this course of world domination, and to join in an historic effort to end the perilous arms race and transform the history of man. He has an opportunity now to move the world back from the abyss of destruction—by returning to his Government's own words that it had no need to station missiles outside its own territory, and withdrawing these weapons from Cuba—by refraining from any action which will widen or deepen the present crisis—and then by participating in a search for peaceful and permanent solutions. . . .

We are prepared to discuss new proposals for the removal of tensions on both sides—including the possibilities of a genuinely independent Cuba, free to determine its own destiny. We have no wish to war with the Soviet Union—for we are a peaceful people who desire to live in peace with all other peoples. . . .

Finally, I want to say a few words to the captive people of Cuba, to whom this speech is being directly carried by special radio facilities. I speak to you as a friend, as one who knows of your deep attachment to your fatherland, as one who shares your aspirations for liberty and justice for all. And I have watched with deep sorrow how your nationalist revolution was betrayed and how your fatherland fell under foreign domination. . . .

My fellow citizens: let no one doubt that this is a difficult and dangerous effort on which we have set out. No one can foresee precisely what course it will take or what costs or casualties will be incurred. Many months of sacrifice and self-discipline lie ahead—months in which both our will and our patience will be tested—months in which many threats and denunciations will keep us aware of our danger. But the greatest danger of all would be to do nothing.

The path we have chosen for the present is full of hazards, as all paths are—but it is the one most consistent with our character and courage as a nation and our commitments around the world. The cost of freedom is always high—but Americans have always paid it. And one path we shall never choose is the path of surrender or submission.

Our goal is not the victory of might but the vindication of right; not peace at the expense of freedom, but both peace and freedom, here in this hemisphere, and, we hope, around the world. God willing, that goal will be achieved.

John F. Kennedy, radio and television address to the nation on the Cuban missile crisis, Washington, D.C., October 22, 1962.

Document 10: The New Frontier and Space

In Kennedy's last major address before his assassination, the president spoke of the need to go to space during the dedication of the Aerospace Medical Health Center in San Antonio, Texas, just one day before being shot in Dallas.

For more than 3 years I have spoken about the New Frontier. This is not a partisan term, and it is not the exclusive property of Republicans or Democrats. It refers, instead, to this Nation's place in history, to the fact that we do stand on the edge of a great new era, filled with both crisis and opportunity, an era to be characterized by achievement and by challenge. It is an era which calls for action and for the best efforts of all those who would test the unknown and the uncertain in every phase of human endeavor. It is a time for pathfinders and pioneers.

I have come to Texas today to salute an outstanding group of pioneers, the men who man the Brooks Air Force Base School of Aerospace Medicine and the Aerospace Medical Center. It is fitting that San Antonio should be the site of this center and this school as we gather to dedicate this complex of buildings. For this city has long been the home of the pioneers in the air. It was here that Sidney Brooks, whose memory we honor today, was born and raised. It was here that Charles Lindbergh and Claire Chennault, and a host of others, who, in World War I and World War II and Korea, and even today have helped demonstrate American mastery of the skies, trained at Kelly Field and Randolph Field, which form a major part of aviation history. And in the new frontier of outer space, while headlines may be made by others in other places, history is being made every day by the men and women of the Aerospace Medical Center, without whom there could be no history.

Many Americans make the mistake of assuming that space research has no value here on earth. Nothing could be further from the truth. Just as the wartime development of radar gave us the transistor, and all that it made possible, so research in space medicine holds the promise of substantial benefit for those of us who are earthbound. For our effort in space is not as some have suggested, a competitor for the natural resources that we need to develop the earth. It is a working partner and a coproducer of these resources. And nothing makes this clearer than the fact that medicine in space is going to make our lives healthier and happier here on earth.

I give you three examples: first, medical space research may open up new understanding of man's relation to his environment. Examinations of the astronaut's physical, and mental, and emotional reactions can teach us more about the differences between normal and abnormal, about the causes and effects of disorientation, about changes in metabolism which could result in extending the life span. When you study the effects on our astronauts of exhaust gases which can contaminate their environment, and you seek ways to alter these gases so as to reduce their toxicity, you are working on problems similar to those in our great urban centers which themselves are being corrupted by gases and which must be clear.

And second, medical space research may revolutionize the technology and the techniques of modern medicine. Whatever new devices are created, for example, to monitor our astronauts, to measure their heart activity, their breathing, their brain waves, their eye motion, at great distances and under difficult conditions, will also represent a major advance in general medical instrumentation. Heart patients may even be able to wear a light monitor which will sound a warning if their activity exceeds certain limits. An instrument recently developed to record automatically the impact of acceleration upon an astronaut's eyes will also be of help to small children who are suffering miserably from eye defects, but are unable to describe their impairment. And also by the use of instruments similar to those used in Project Mercury, this Nation's private as well as public nursing services are being improved, enabling one nurse now to give more critically ill patients greater attention than they ever could in the past.

And third, medical space research may lead to new safeguards against hazards common to many environments. Specifically, our astronauts will need fundamentally new devices to protect them from the ill effects of radiation which can have a profound influence upon medicine and man's relations to our present environment.

Here at this center we have the laboratories, the talent, the resources to give new impetus to vital research in the life centers. I am not suggesting that the entire space program is justified alone by what is done in medicine. The space program stands on its own as a contribution to national strength. And last Saturday at Cape Canaveral I saw our new

Saturn C-1 rocket booster, which, with its payload, when it rises in December of this year, will be, for the first time, the largest booster in the world, carrying into space the largest payload that any country in the world has ever sent into space.

I think the United States should be a leader. A country as rich and powerful as this which bears so many burdens and responsibilities, which has so many opportunities, should be second to none. And in December, while I do not regard our mastery of space as anywhere near complete, while I recognize that there are still areas where we are behind—at least in one area, the size of the booster—this year I hope the United States will be ahead. And I am for it. We have a long way to go. Many weeks and months and years of long, tedious work lie ahead. There will be setbacks and frustrations and disappointments. There will be, as there always are, pressures in this country to do less in this area as in so many others, and temptations to do something else that is perhaps easier. But this research here must go on. This space effort must go on. The conquest of space must and will go ahead. That much we know. That much we can say with confidence and conviction.

Frank O'Connor, the Irish writer, tells in one of his books how, as a boy, he and his friends would make their way across the countryside, and when they came to an orchard wall that seemed too high and too doubtful to try and too difficult to permit their voyage to continue, they took off their hats and tossed them over the wall—and then they had no choice but to follow them.

This Nation has tossed its cap over the wall of space, and we have no choice but to follow it. Whatever the difficulties, they will be overcome. Whatever the hazards, they must be guarded against. With the vital help of this Aerospace Medical Center, with the help of all those who labor in the space endeavor, with the help and support of all Americans, we will climb this wall with safety and with speed—and we shall then explore the wonders on the other side.

John F. Kennedy, speech at the dedication of the Aerospace Medical Health Center, San Antonio, Texas, November 21, 1963.

Chronology

1917

John Fitzgerald "Jack" Kennedy is born on May 29 to Rose Fitzgerald Kennedy and Joseph P. Kennedy in Brookline, Massachusetts.

1929

The American stock market collapses; Joseph Kennedy moves his family to Bronxville, New York, and buys a vacation home for the family in Hyannis Port, Massachusetts.

1930

Kennedy begins school at the Canterbury School.

1931

Kennedy continues his education at the Choate School.

1935

Kennedy graduates from Choate; he travels to Europe and Latin America and then enrolls in Princeton University.

1936

Kennedy transfers from Princeton to Harvard University.

1938

Kennedy's father, Joseph, is appointed the U.S. ambassador to Great Britain.

1939

German aggression starts World War II.

1940

Kennedy graduates from Harvard. His senior thesis, *Why England Slept*, is published and gains him a degree of notoriety. Kennedy's father resigns his ambassadorship.

1941
Japan attacks Pearl Harbor in Hawaii, and the United States enters World War II.

1943
PT-109, under Kennedy's command, is sunk in the South Pacific by a Japanese destroyer on August 2; Kennedy saves the crew and becomes a hero.

1945
Kennedy is discharged from the navy and finds employment as a news correspondent for Hearst newspapers.

1946
Against a crowded field of candidates, Kennedy wins the Democratic primary for Massachusetts's Eleventh Congressional District. He is elected to Congress in November.

1952
Kennedy wins his bid for the U.S. Senate against well-known incumbent Henry Cabot Lodge Jr.

1953
Kennedy marries Jacqueline Bouvier on September 12 in Newport, Rhode Island.

1955
Kennedy writes *Profiles in Courage*, which becomes a best-seller.

1956
Kennedy attempts but fails to secure the Democratic nomination for vice president.

1957
Kennedy serves on the Senate Foreign Relations Committee; he wins the Pulitzer Prize in biography for *Profiles in Courage*; and his daughter, Caroline, is born.

1958
Kennedy is reelected to the U.S. Senate by a large margin.

1960

Kennedy shows poise in a televised presidential debate against Richard Nixon on September 26; Kennedy is elected president. His son John Fitzgerald Jr. is born.

JANUARY 1961

On January 20, Kennedy is inaugurated as the thirty-fifth president of the United States. His inaugural address, announcing the New Frontier program and calling on Americans to "ask not what your country can do for you; ask what you can do for your country," is considered one of the best ever. Later that month he signs executive orders increasing the quantity of surplus food distributed to jobless Americans and expanding the Food for Peace program to reduce hunger in other nations.

MARCH 1961

Kennedy creates the Peace Corps via an executive order and proposes the Alliance for Progress initiative between Latin America and the United States.

APRIL 17–19, 1961

The Bay of Pigs invasion of Cuba fails.

MAY 1961

Alan Shepard becomes the first American in space, and Kennedy sets the goal of putting a man on the moon before the end of the decade.

JUNE 3, 1961

Kennedy and Soviet premier Nikita Khrushchev meet in Vienna, Austria.

JULY 1961

Kennedy aids West Berlin in response to the Soviet construction of the Berlin Wall.

APRIL 1962

Kennedy is successful in getting U.S. Steel to end price increases.

SEPTEMBER 30, 1962

Kennedy authorizes federal troops to escort the first black student enrolled at the University of Mississippi.

OCTOBER 1962

Kennedy orders a naval blockade to stop the Soviet attempt to place missiles in Cuba.

NOVEMBER 20, 1962

Kennedy signs an executive order to prohibit segregation in federally funded housing programs.

FEBRUARY 28, 1963

Kennedy proposes a major civil rights initiative.

JUNE 11, 1963

Kennedy mobilizes the Alabama National Guard to escort the first two black students admitted to the University of Alabama. Kennedy reforms and restructures tax system.

JUNE 22, 1963

In an address to the nation, Kennedy discusses his proposal for sweeping civil rights legislation.

JUNE 26, 1963

While touring Europe, Kennedy delivers an address in Berlin, condemning communism with his statement that "freedom has many difficulties and democracy is not perfect, but we have never had to put a wall up to keep our people in."

JULY 26, 1963

Kennedy proposes the Nuclear Arms Test Ban Treaty.

AUGUST 9, 1963

Kennedy's son Patrick Bouvier dies after premature birth.

OCTOBER 1963

Senate begins debate on Kennedy's plan to cut taxes in order to stimulate the economy.

OCTOBER 7, 1963

Kennedy and Soviet premier Khrushchev sign the Limited Nuclear Test Ban Treaty.

NOVEMBER 22, 1963

Kennedy is assassinated by Lee Harvey Oswald in Dallas, Texas. Vice President Lyndon B. Johnson is sworn in as the thirty-sixth president of the United States.

NOVEMBER 25, 1963

After a state funeral, Kennedy is buried in Arlington National Cemetery.

FOR FURTHER RESEARCH

GENERAL BIOGRAPHY

LETITIA BALDRIDGE, *In the Kennedy Style.* New York: Doubleday, 1998.

JIM BISHOP, *A Day in the Life of President Kennedy.* New York: Franklin Watts, 1962.

BENJAMIN C. BRADLEE, *Conversations with Kennedy.* New York: W.W. Norton, 1975.

DAVID BRUNER, *John F. Kennedy and a New Generation.* Boston: Little, Brown, 1988.

ROBERT DONOVAN, *"PT 109": John F. Kennedy in World War II.* Greenwich, CT: Fawcett, 1961.

PHILIP B. KUNHARDT JR., ED., *Life in Camelot: The Kennedy Years.* Boston: Little, Brown, 1988.

VICTOR LASKY, *JFK: The Man and the Myth.* New York: Macmillan, 1963.

I.E. LEVINE, *The Young Man in the White House: John Fitzgerald Kennedy.* New York: Julian Messner, 1964.

WILLIAM MANCHESTER, *The Death of a President.* New York: Harper & Row, 1967.

JUDE MILLS, *John F. Kennedy.* New York: Franklin Watts, 1962.

RICHARD REEVES, *President Kennedy: Profile of Power.* New York: Simon & Schuster, 1993.

ARTHUR M. SCHLESINGER JR., *A Thousand Days: John F. Kennedy in the White House.* Boston: Houghton Mifflin, 1963.

PETER SCHWAB AND J. LEE SHNUDMAN, *John F. Kennedy.* Boston: Twayne, 1974.

HUGH SIDEY, *John F. Kennedy, President.* New York: Atheneum, 1964.

The Bay of Pigs Invasion and the Cuban Missile Crisis

James Blight and Peter Kornbluth, eds., *Politics of Illusion: The Bay of Pigs Invasion Reexamined.* Boulder, CO: Lynne Rienner, 1998.

Raymond Garthoff, *Reflections on the Cuban Missile Crisis.* Washington, DC: Brookings Institution, 1987.

Trumbull Higgins, *The Perfect Failure: Kennedy, Eisenhower, and the CIA at the Bay of Pigs.* New York: W.W. Norton, 1987.

Roger Hilsman, *The Cuban Missile Crisis: The Struggle over Policy.* Westport, CT: Praeger, 1996.

Robert F. Kennedy, *The Thirteen Days: A Memoir of the Cuban Missile Crisis.* New York: W.W. Norton, 1969.

Peter Kornbluth, ed., *The Bay of Pigs Declassified: The Secret CIA Report on the Invasion of Cuba.* New York: New Press, 1998.

James A. Nathan, *Anatomy of the Cuban Missile Crisis.* Westport, CT: Greenwood, 2001.

Michael Weisbrot, *Maximum Danger: Kennedy, the Missiles, and the Crisis of American Confidence.* Chicago: Ivan R. Dee, 2001.

Mark White, *The Cuban Missile Crisis.* Basingstoke, NH: Macmillan, 1996.

Peter Wyden, *Bay of Pigs: The Untold Story.* New York: Simon & Schuster, 1979.

Kennedy's Foreign Policy

Michael Beschloss, *The Crisis Years: Kennedy and Khrushchev, 1960–1963.* New York: Edward Burlingame Books, 1991.

Lawrence Freedman, *Kennedy's Wars: Berlin, Cuba, Laos, and Vietnam.* New York: Oxford University Press, 2000.

David Kaiser, *American Tragedy: Kennedy, Johnson, and the Origins of the Vietnam War.* Cambridge, MA: Belknap, 2000.

RICHARD J. WALTON, *Cold War and Counterrevolution: The Foreign Policy of John F. Kennedy.* New York: Viking, 1972.

KENNEDY'S DOMESTIC POLICY

IRVING BERNSTEIN, *Promises Kept: John F. Kennedy's New Frontier.* New York: Oxford University Press, 1991.

THOMAS CLARKIN, *Federal Indian Policy in the Kennedy and Johnson Administrations, 1961–1969.* Albuquerque: University of New Mexico Press, 2001.

MARK STERN, *Calculating Visions: Kennedy, Johnson, and Civil Rights.* New Brunswick, NJ: Rutgers University Press, 1992.

BOOKS BY KENNEDY

JOHN F. KENNEDY, *Profiles in Courage.* New York: Harper & Row, 1955.

———, *Why England Slept.* New York: Funk, 1961.

WEBSITES

AMERICAN PRESIDENTS: LIFE PORTRAITS, www.americanpresidents.org. Based on the popular C-SPAN series of the same name, this site contains facts on Kennedy, his inaugural address, and links to other resources and related sites. Visitors to the site may view segments of the popular series featuring important events in Kennedy's life.

THE JOHN F. KENNEDY ASSASSINATION HOMEPAGE, www.jfk-assassination.de. This website features the Warren Commission report and hearings on the assassination; a list of books and sources on Kennedy; photos of the motorcade route, bullet, and assassin; films on the tragic event; and an assortment of facts, myths, and information on the assassination.

JOHN F. KENNEDY LIBRARY AND MUSEUM, www.cs.umb.edu/jfklibrary. One of the institutions in the presidential library system, the Kennedy Library houses the most comprehensive collection of Kennedy holdings, including speeches, books, presidential papers, photos, sound recordings, and oral histories.

INDEX

Brazil, 99
Brookline, Massachusetts, 12
Brown, Seyom, 22, 50, 81
B-26 aircraft, 40, 46
B-29 aircraft, 161
Bundy, McGeorge, 20, 69, 73, 159
Burner, David, 163
Burns, James MacGregor, 16
Bush, Vannevar, 161
By Weight of Arms: America's Overseas Military Policy (1969 study), 41–43

Cambodia, 75
Cannon, Clarence D., 180–82
Canterbury School (Connecticut), 14
Cape Canaveral, Florida, 173
Cape Cod, Massachusetts, 13
Carey, Robert G., 109
Castro, Fidel, 18, 22, 35–37, 68, 95
  awareness of CIA plans for guerrilla action and, 38, 46
  Kennedy's reluctance to use American military to overthrow, 23
  Soviet Union as ally of, 39
  support of Cuban population for, 41
Central Intelligence Agency (CIA), 21, 44, 76, 111
  plans for Bay of Pigs invasion and, 23, 41, 45, 46
    ineptitude of, revealed to press, 47
    optimism about, 95
    training of Cuban exiles for guerrilla action and, 37–38
Chicago Daily News, 204
Choate (boarding school), 14, 15
Civilian Conservation Corps, 109
civil rights, 29–31, 43, 127
  African American expectations and, 125
  caution in Kennedy's approach to, 129
  apparent reluctance to act and, 144, 147
    disappointment of African Americans about, 134–35
    minimal interest and, 137, 139
    pragmatism and, 138
    until pushed to action, 140, 146
  Freedom Riders and, 30, 131, 141, 143
  Kennedy's support for, 132–33
  growing demand for, 136

international problems a distraction from, for Kennedy, 128, 130
  Kennedy's legacy and, 146–47
  as moral issue, 145
  symbolic and legal actions for, 142
  see also desegregation
Civil Rights Act (1957), 138
Civil Rights Bill (1963), 31, 144–46
Civil Rights Commission, U.S., 129–30, 135, 139, 157
civil rights movement, 146
Clay, Lucius, 58, 59
Clemson University, 157
Clinch, Nancy Gager, 35
Clinton, Bill, 32
Coast Guard Academy, 29
Cold War, 18, 51, 59, 66, 161
  aid policy influenced by, 84–85
  Kennedy's attempt to move beyond, 82
  Kennedy's attitude toward, 21, 22
Cold War and Counterrevolution: The Foreign Policy of John F. Kennedy (Walton), 48, 86
Cold War Years: American Foreign Policy Since 1945 (Hammond), 98–99
Committee on Equal Employment Opportunity, 29
communism, 69, 77, 86
  aid programs intended to counter, 81–83, 87, 90
  failure of American leaders to understand attraction of, 68–69
  Kennedy's stance against, 42, 68, 79, 93, 201
  seen as threat, 95, 128
    in Latin America, 84–85
    reflexive reaction of Americans and, 78
  space program and, 172–73
  U.S. policy debates and, 36–37
  in Vietnam, 72, 73
Congress of Racial Equality (CORE), 130–32
Congress, U.S., 28, 42, 56, 72, 165
  aid programs and, 25, 86, 98, 103, 118
  civil rights and, 31, 129, 132, 138
  Kennedy's election to, 16–17
  Medicare health system and, 29
  space program and, 162, 180, 182
Connecticut, 14
Connor, "Bull," 144

About the Editors

Tom Lansford, Ph.D., is assistant professor of political science at the University of Southern Mississippi and a fellow with the Frank Maria Center for International Politics and Ethics. He has published dozens of scholarly articles and chapters. Among his books are *All for One: Terrorism, NATO, and the United States* (2002) and *The Lords of Foggy Bottom: The American Secretaries of State and the World They Shaped* (2001).

Robert P. Watson, Ph.D., is associate professor of political science at Florida Atlantic University and editor of the journal *White House Studies.* He is the author or editor of sixteen books, including *The Presidents' Wives: Reassessing the Office of the First Lady* (2000), and has published more than one hundred scholarly articles and essays.

Both Lansford and Watson have convened national conferences on the presidency and serve on the boards of numerous scholarly associations and journals. The two have written several books together, including Greenhaven Press's *Presidents and Their Decisions: Theodore Roosevelt.*